Whether you are all in on the plant-based lifestyle or you're just a little bit plant-curious, you'll find the vegan cakes of your dreams in *Plantcakes*. Inside are recipes for cakes of all shapes and sizes, to fill any craving or occasion—from a rainy Wednesday slice of emotional eating, to a spectacular sheet cake for a crowd, to show-stopping party cakes with major flair. You'll never be short of options with chapters on:

SNACKING CAKES
When you need to snack and you need to snack now, whip up the Orange Citrus Cake, Blueberry Sour Cream Streusel Cake, or Vanilla Cake with Coffee Icing Glaze.

TWO-LAYER CAKES
Keep it casual cool with cakes like the Dark Chocolate Cake with Chocolate Fudge Buttercream, Supermarket Bakery–Style Cake with Pink Vanilla Buttercream, or Vanilla Almond Raspberry Cake.

THREE-LAYER CAKES
When you feel like getting fancy, there's the Coffee Milk Cake with Coffee Swiss Meringue Buttercream, Passion Fruit Vanilla Bean Ombré Cake, or PB+J Chocolate Cake with Peanut Butter Cup Crunch.

PARTY TIME (OR EVERYDAY) CUPCAKES
When cupcakes are called for, try the Garden Party Vanilla Lemon Cupcakes, Blackberry Almond Cupcakes, or "They Don't Know They're Healthy" Banana Chocolate Chip Cupcakes.

WILDCARD CAKES
And to really take the cake, turn to the Abstract-Painted Buttercream Blackberry Cake with Meringue Kisses, Giant Chocolate Chip Cookie Cake, Black Sesame Brittle Cake, or Mocha Dacquoise Cake.

With step-by-step instructions, easy-to-find ingredients, and accessible plant-based alternatives for all the usual baking essentials, *Plantcakes* makes vegan baking a breeze. Whether you've never baked before or are an experienced baker ready to explore the vegan side, you're bound to learn a thing or two—like how to make the best buttercream ever (without the butter!) or some sweet piping techniques—from self-taught baker, Lyndsay Sung, creator of the wildly popular cake making and decorating site, *Coco Cake Land*.

In addition to the recipes, the book's eye-popping photography leaps right off the page, and its vibrant, kaleidoscopic design brings everything together in one irresistibly sweet package. *Plantcakes* is the perfect gift for all the plant-based and plant-curious people in your life, bringing cake to the people in the most delightful, plant-based way. Let's all eat (vegan) cake!

PLANTCAKES

FANCY + EVERYDAY VEGAN CAKES FOR EVERYONE

LYNDSAY SUNG

CREATOR OF COCO CAKE LAND

Copyright © 2023 Lyndsay Sung

All rights reserved. The use of any part of this publication, reproduced, transmitted in any form or by any means electronic, mechanical, photocopying, recording or otherwise, or stored in a retrieval system without the prior written consent of the publisher—or in the case of photocopying or other reprographic copying, license from the Canadian Copyright Licensing Agency—is an infringement of the copyright law.

Appetite by Random House® and colophon are registered trademarks of Penguin Random House LLC.

Library and Archives Canada Cataloguing in Publication is available upon request.
ISBN: 978-0-52-561183-7
eBook ISBN: 978-0-52-561184-4

Photography by Lyndsay Sung
Cover and book design by Jennifer Griffiths
Printed in China

Published in Canada by Appetite by Random House®, a division of Penguin Random House Canada Limited

www.penguinrandomhouse.ca

10 9 8 7 6 5 4 3 2 1

appetite by RANDOM HOUSE | Penguin Random House Canada

To my two sweet fellows—my husband, Rich, and my son, Teddy—you two are my very favorite.

CONTENTS

Introduction *1*
Plant-Based Ingredients *5*
Cool Tools *11*
Hot Tips *15*
How to Fill + Frost a Cake *19*
Put It in Your Bag + Pipe It *25*
Finishing Touches . . . *37*

1

SNACKING CAKES FOR EMOTIONAL EATING (+ JUST REGULAR EATING)

Apple Olive Oil Cake with Maple Cream Cheese Frosting *42*
Blackberry Maple Breakfast Cake with Maple Coconut Whipped Cream *45*
Chocolate Almond Brownie Cake with Vanilla Buttercream (GF) *47*
Lemon Loaf Cake with Vanilla Bean Glaze *51*
Cozy Pumpkin Pie Cake *52*
Blueberry Sour Cream Streusel Cake *55*
Orange Citrus Cake with Orange Juice Glaze *57*
Peanut Butter Snacking Cake with Caramel Frosting *61*
Vanilla Cake with Coffee Icing Glaze *63*

2

"A LITTLE MORE CASUAL" TWO-LAYER CAKES

Banana Cake with Peanut Butter Frosting *69*
Dark Chocolate Cake with Chocolate Fudge Buttercream *78*
Strawberries and Cream Strawberry Jam Cake *71*
Vanilla Almond Raspberry Cake with Vanilla Buttercream + Caramel Almond Brittle (GF) *73*
Supermarket Bakery–Style Cake with Pink Vanilla Buttercream *75*

3

PARTY ANIMAL THREE-LAYER CAKES

Apple Caramel Cake with Oatmeal Cookie Crumbles *83*
Banana Caramel Cake with Salted Caramel Buttercream + Caramel Drips *85*
Passion Fruit Vanilla Bean Ombré Cake with Caramel Crunch *89*
Funfetti Cake with Vanilla Buttercream and Birthday Cake Crumbles *91*
Vanilla Fruit + Flowers Cake with Vanilla Bean Swiss Meringue Buttercream *95*
Strawberry Dream Cake with Strawberry Swiss Meringue Buttercream *99*
Cookies and Cream Cake *101*
Coffee Milk Cake with Coffee Swiss Meringue Buttercream + Raspberries *105*
PB+J Chocolate Cake with Peanut Butter Cup Crunch *107*
Easy Chocolate Cake with Chocolate Ganache Frosting *110*
Party Time Chocolate Raspberry Ruffle Cake *112*
Chocolate Hazelnut Cake with Candied Hazelnuts *115*

4
BUTTERCREAM DREAMS (FILLINGS + FROSTINGS, + ONE VERY BERRY QUICK JAM)

Classic Buttercreams 125

Swiss Meringue Buttercreams 129

Italian Meringue Buttercreams 135

Other Frostings + One Very Berry Quick Jam 139

5
FANCIFUL WILDCARD CAKES (TRULY OUTRAGEOUS)

Giant Chocolate Chip Cookie Cake with Vanilla Buttercream 145

Fancy Breakfast Cake with Maple Italian Meringue Buttercream, Coffee Syrup + Blueberry Jam 149

Dance Like No One Is Watching Earl Grey Cake with Lemon Italian Meringue Buttercream 151

Holiday Vibes Chocolate Stump Cake 155

Black Sesame Brittle Cake with Coconut Swiss Meringue Buttercream 159

Matcha Green Tea Cake with Raspberry Buttercream + Matcha Mini Cookies 161

Mocha Dacquoise Cake 164

Pistachio Cake with Strawberry Swiss Meringue Buttercream 169

Cotton Candy Cake with Watercolor Buttercream 171

Abstract-Painted Buttercream Blackberry Cake with Meringue Kisses 177

6
FANCY SHEET CAKES (TO FEED A CROWD)

Buttercream Flower Garden Holy Sheet Cake 182

Coconut Haupia Cake with Passion Fruit Syrup 187

Carrot Pineapple Sheet Cake with Tangy Yogurt Frosting 191

Lemon Coconut Cake with Lemon Swiss Meringue Buttercream 193

Pressed Flower Funfetti Cake Bars 195

Raspberry Lemon Sheet Cake with Raspberry Italian Meringue Buttercream 199

Tie-Dye Rainbow Piped Buttercream Cake 201

7
PARTY TIME (OR EVERYDAY) CUPCAKES

Birthday Cupcakes with Strawberry Frosting 207

Blackberry Almond Cupcakes with Vanilla Blackberry Jam Frosting 208

Garden Party Vanilla Lemon Cupcakes 210

The "They Don't Know They're Healthy" Banana Chocolate Chip Cupcakes 213

Chocolate Chip Cupcakes 215

Chocolate Cupcakes with Peanut Butter Frosting 219

Chocolate Party Time Cupcakes 220

Acknowledgements 223

Resources 225

Index 228

INTRODUCTION

Hello there, old and new friends, and welcome to *Plantcakes!* You may remember me from *Coco Cake Land*—the blog, the book, the persona—a colorful buttercream-frosted world of cute animal cakes, piped flowers, gentle jokes, and all-around good times, with a delightfully friendly side of feminism. Since starting *Coco Cake Land*, I have baked and decorated thousands of cakes of all flavors, shapes, and sizes, but in the last few years I've pretty much got obsessed with plant-based baking. It's become like a personal challenge to me: can I make absolutely delicious and beautiful cakes, designed and decorated in my *Coco Cake Land* style, that are completely plant-based too? It turns out that yes, I can! And I'm so excited to share the recipes with you in this book!

Plantcakes is a book for everyone who loves cake. Whether you're fully plant-based, or you're plant-forward, plant-curious, or plant-adjacent, this book will give all plant people the confidence you need to make a beautiful plant-based, buttercream-frosted cake for the special folks in your life—and yourself!

When I refer to my plant people, I mean those who are:

PLANT LOVERS: Eating 100%-plant-based foods.

PLANT-FORWARD: Eating a majority of plant-based foods, and making daily choices that almost always include plant-based eating.

PLANT-CURIOUS: Discovering the delicious joys of plant-based eating, and making a conscious shift in eating patterns toward it.

PLANT-ADJACENT: Have family members or close friends/loved ones/partners who are plant-based and want to be able to make them delicious, beautiful plant-based cakes.

PLANT DISCOVERIES

Many folks decide to try plant-based eating for a myriad of factors, including animal welfare, environmental concerns, food restrictions, or health reasons. I believe that the more we can influence people to make plant-based choices, the better—and my philosophy is to try to do that in an encouraging, positive, and delicious way. I call myself "majority plant-forward" because mine is a primarily vegetarian family, and many of the meals we eat at home are also vegan. I still remember when I first learned about veganism—I was in my early twenties and living with my best bud roommate during university. By then I'd already been through several "lazy vegetarian" phases, yet I knew very little about cooking or nutrition. Lunch would be opening up a can of cream of mushroom soup and heating its gloopy contents on the stovetop, or making toast with peanut butter, or pouring a bowl of cereal. My roommate's partner at the time was vegan, and a kitschy, colorful book called *How It All Vegan!* showed up in our living room one day. I started reading through it, drawn in by the cute retro 1950s vibes. I had never ever thought about removing animal products completely before—they were simply a part of my life, seemingly as natural as tying a shoe. Upon reading *How It All Vegan!* though, my fragile little mind was blown. I liked the non-judgmental and encouraging nature of the book, all about the most earth-friendly things you could do—like how they suggested not to throw out your leather belt or shoes, but to continue to use them until they're completely worn, and then replace them with your future, plant-based choice, so as not to be wasteful. It opened my eyes to another way of thinking, and it definitely piqued my curiosity about veganism.

A few years later, I went on my first date with my now husband, Rich. With his faded black jean jacket, red Converse sneakers and Tin Tin hair, he was very cute, very cool, and . . . very vegan. This was intimidating to me, and I remember being terrified to eat anything that wasn't vegan around him—even though he is such a gentle, non-judgmental, and open soul. (Our first few months of dating featured lots of peanut butter on celery sticks!) Back then, over two decades ago, finding delicious vegan things to eat in stores or restaurants was not easy. Nowadays, being plant-based or vegan is so common that no one bats an eye, and plant-based eating has exploded with delicious options all over. The days of wondering "what do vegans eat" are long gone— one quick Google search will yield millions of hits for amazing plant-based meals— and food companies both large and small are following suit by expanding their offerings. Feel like eating a plant-based burger and fries? You can drive through a fast-food chain in any major city now and satisfy your craving. Supermarket aisles have dedicated sections for plant-based products, and the dairy cooler is stocked with plant milk and dairy-free butter alternatives.

My dear friend Sharon has been a huge inspiration to me in plant-based eating. Sharon has been vegan since forever, and always has the most delicious food at her parties—cheeseballs, pâté, lasagna, desserts. Encouraged by her, I've been adjusting and "plantifying" recipes for many years now (my favorite veganized dishes include a karaage-style fried "chicken" made with twice-frozen-twice-thawed tofu, and my latest Chinese comfort-food creation, BBQ pork buns made with marinated seitan caramelized in the oven, then stuffed into white steamed-to-juicy-soft-bunned-perfection bao), including some desserts, and it was Sharon who first inspired me to experiment with "plantifying" my cake recipes too. It's been a fun personal challenge to create super delicious plant-based cakes that everyone can happily enjoy, all without anyone noticing they are vegan!

Plantcakes falls within the same non-judgmental and encouraging parameters in which plant-based eating was introduced to me. Perhaps you, like many others, have realized how easy and delicious it is to be vegan or eat more plant-forwardly! Or maybe making more plant-based choices is something you're curious about, or it's reflective of how you naturally tend to eat and you'd like to learn more. Wherever you are on your plant-based journey, this book is for you!

IT'S ALL IN THE ATTITUDE
As a child, I heard that more times than I could count. My mom loved to say it when I was having a grump attack, or when I was nervous about starting something new. Of course, now I find myself saying it to my son, Teddy, all the time—because it's true! A positive attitude can really make the difference in life. As a cancer survivor, I know this to be true—trying to keep positive and finding the twisted humor through cancer treatment helped buoy me up, and being appreciative of life's many gifts is something I've learned through experience. Life is precious, and it will fly by, and the days will pass no matter what—so you may as well try to live it with an easy laugh. Thankfully, delicious cake has the ability to put a smile on quite a few faces.

If you've never baked before, it can feel intimidating at first. My advice is to start with a simple snacking cake—a single-layer cake iced

WHEREVER YOU ARE ON YOUR PLANT-BASED

with an easy glaze or frosting. Baking can be so satisfying because it feels like a mini achievement (or sometimes a gargantuan achievement!) when your cake comes out springy and soft and your kitchen smells like warm vanilla. From the snacking cake, you can work up to two-layer cakes, then

JOURNEY, THIS BOOK IS FOR YOU!

graduate to a three-layer showstopper! Don't worry if your early attempts at baking don't end up as you imagined—try, try, and try again. Practice makes better and perhaps eventually, perfect(ish). I *still* bomb in the kitchen sometimes, and heck, this is my second published cake book. Plus, if a cake looks like garbage, you can always add lots of sprinkles to cover it up, hehe, and it will likely still taste great.

Whether it's a tender-crumbed funfetti vanilla cake with buttercream frosting, or a moist chocolate cake layered with chocolate ganache frosting, or cupcakes with buttercream piped flowers for a special birthday or bake sale, *Plantcakes* has the goods to make your special celebration—or just a random Wednesday night—a real treat! I hope you have fun with *Plantcakes*—and that it brings joy to you and your loved ones in the form of soft, moist cake and creamy frosting. As I like to remind myself, life is short, enjoy the good times, treasure your loved ones, choose kindness . . . and eat that caaaaaake!

Happy cake making to you!

XO Lyndsay

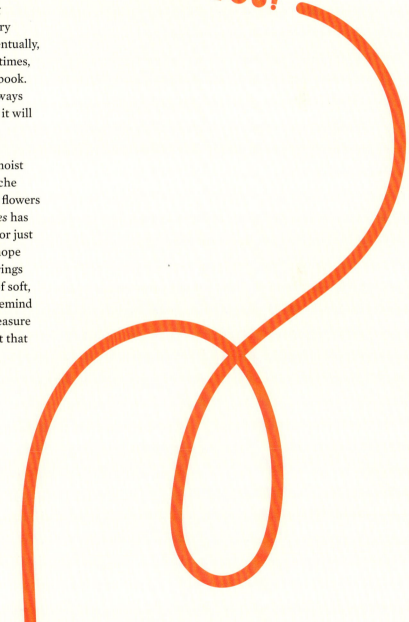

INTRODUCTION 3

PLANT-BASED INGREDIENTS

When choosing ingredients, you can go low or you can go high. If you want an all-organic cake, you can certainly achieve that—organic flour and sugar, organic plant-based milk and butter, even organic vegetable shortening! If you want a delicious cake made with ingredients that won't break the bank, then you don't need to spend a fortune either. I get so excited when I hear about new plant-based ingredients to try in my baking, or discover something new at the grocery store. Keep in mind, though, that some vegan ingredients may still have social or environmental impacts, so research the companies that make these ingredients, and buy products that best align with your personal values.

AQUAFABA

Detailed on page 8, aquafaba is the thick, viscous egg-white-like liquid from a can of chickpeas that usually gets poured down the drain but to my mind is LIQUID GOLD! Especially for making plant-based meringue buttercreams and Meringue Kisses (page 177). If you have an allergy to beans (and therefore aquafaba), you can try using Versawhip for an alternative (read more on page 9).

BUTTER

There are so many great choices for plant-based butters these days! I recommend using unsalted butter for all my recipes, so be aware of added salt and adjust the recipe accordingly. For making buttercreams, I recommend a firm, unsalted brick-style butter such as Becel unsalted or Flora unsalted plant-based butter. Miyoko's Creamery organic vegan butter is also delicious, and it's made from cashews and coconut oil. (I try to snag the more expensive butters when they go on sale and then freeze them.) Earth Balance buttery sticks are also a readily available plant-based butter with a reasonable price point. Check out what your local store has in stock and experiment with the butter flavor you like best, as there are so many options these days. Note that some plant-based butters can be more melty than others, so keep an eye on it as it comes to room temperature and use it promptly. For more about choosing butter for buttercream, see page 121.

CHOCOLATE

Like any ingredient, there can be a range of choices in both quality and price, and this is definitely true for chocolate. On the modestly priced end of the spectrum, you can find popular brands of vegan and dairy-free semisweet, bittersweet, and dark chocolate bars and chocolate chips at the supermarket for use in plant-based baking, including the Kirkland brand semisweet chocolate chips at Costco. On the more expensive end, you can explore the larger and more readily available range of premium and artisan chocolate brands, such as Callebaut, Guittard, and Valrhona, for their dairy-free chocolate options. It's always worthwhile to see what's available locally too, to help support local chocolate makers! For special-occasion cakes, it can be worth it to splurge on high-quality ingredients—seek out the chocolate that meets your personal needs and budget.

COLORINGS

For coloring your cakes and frostings, you can find all sorts of food coloring options. Gel color can be found in specialty cake decorating or gourmet shops, craft superstores, and online. Natural gel color is also an option, as are natural food coloring powders made from fruits and vegetables—see the Resources section (page 225) for where to find those. Most gel color is vegan, but double check the ingredients or contact the manufacturer when in doubt.

FLAVORINGS

Pure vanilla extract is my go-to (see opposite), but coffee extract and cotton candy extract can also add flavor boosts to your cakes. Just be mindful of amounts, as some extracts can be very powerful.

FLOUR

For the majority of the layer cakes in this book, I use cake flour, a finely milled lighter flour that produces a tender cake texture. If you don't have cake flour, you can use all-purpose flour instead: for each cup of all-purpose flour you use, replace 2 tbsp of the flour with 2 tbsp of cornstarch, whisking it into the flour to combine. If you have a gluten allergy, you can try using your favorite gluten-free 1-to-1 baking flour replacement, such as Bob's Red Mill gluten-free baking flour, in all of the recipes in this book. Plus I have a few almond flour–only cakes featured too.

FLOWERS

Edible flowers are one of my secret cake-decorating weapons! Look for organic edible flowers at your local farmers' market and in the herb section of the grocery store, or grow a little pot on your windowsill! Popular and more readily available edible flowers include violets, orchids, bachelor's buttons, and marigolds. I proudly grew nasturtiums from seed one year, but then was bummed when they got eaten through by aphids! Nasturtium leaves look so cool too with their modern shape, but be careful as they are SPICY! In pots, you can easily grow violets, bachelor's buttons, and marigolds—just add water and send a little prayer to the Sun goddess. Read more about using edible flowers to decorate your cakes on page 38.

FRUIT

For cake recipes that use fresh fruit, I choose organic when possible—and always for strawberries and raspberries, and for lemons when zesting and juicing—as the flavors can be sweeter and more pronounced. Frozen fruit is wonderful too! I love to stock up on local fruit during the summer months and freeze it for use throughout the whole dang year! Just be sure to thaw frozen fruit before using it in any of the recipes in this book.

JAM

When I'm trimming a cake and snacking on cake leftovers, I almost always slather a big old dollop of Bonne Maman jam on top (you know the jars with the cute little gingham-patterned lids?). My pantry is filled with Bonne Maman jars repurposed for spices, yeast, and nuts, and they're also great for shaking up and then storing homemade vinaigrettes in the fridge. However, when summer rolls around and all those gorgeous glimmering berries are staring up at me from roadside stands and farmers' markets, or ripe and ready to be plucked from their bushes, I love to make my own jam. Find my go-to jam recipe for any kind of fruit on page 141.

MILK

Full-fat coconut milk was my go-to in my early days of veganizing cake recipes because its rich flavor and fat content adds a lush moistness to cakes (I love Aroy-D brand for both their coconut milk and cream). Coconut milk is still one of my favorite ingredients, but the flavor can be fairly noticeable, so you'll find it's used judiciously in the recipes in this book. You'll see soy milk listed as my plant milk of choice for most of the recipes. Generally, this can be used interchangeably with other plant milks, like almond or oat. Personally, although I love the sweet taste of oat milk, I like the higher fat content of soy milk, so I lean more toward soy. For baking, always choose unflavored plant milks, often marked as "original flavor," so you can control the cake flavor with things like vanilla or other flavor extracts.

NUTS

I'm nuts about nuts—I just love 'em! When using nuts in your cakes, go for organic, roasted nuts for the most flavor. If you have a nut allergy, be aware that some plant-based butter products use cashews, including Miyoko's Creamery butter.

SALT

Salt comes in a variety of grinds and textures—fine, coarse, flakes. For the recipes in this book, I use fine sea salt, which has the same consistency as fine table salt. You can use fine sea salt or table salt interchangeably in any of the recipes. Flaky sea salt is used as a finish on some cakes, like the Peanut Butter Snacking Cake with Caramel Frosting (page 61).

SUGAR

A simple way to ensure your sugar is vegan is by choosing organic sugar, as some non-organic sugars are processed using animal products. You can contact the manufacturer directly to find out for sure.

THICKENERS

Tapioca starch, arrowroot starch, potato starch, and cornstarch are sometimes added to help thicken and stabilize cake batters, frostings, and meringues, or are added to creams to help give them a whipped or thickened consistency.

VANILLA

Pure vanilla extract is my go-to, and one of my favorites is from Rodelle Kitchen. They also make vanilla bean paste and sell whole vanilla bean pods, and making your own extract from the pods is easy too! Split open five or six vanilla bean pods and place them in a bottle or jar filled with one cup (250 ml) of vodka. Let it sit for a minimum of six months, and you have made your own vanilla!

VEGETABLE SHORTENING

Vegetable shortening is the key to that classic supermarket bakery frosting—plus, it's very temperature stable and won't melt on you as easily as butter, and can add stability to meringue-based buttercreams. My favorite is Spectrum brand organic vegetable shortening. It is a little pricier, but good quality with no discernible flavor. More readily available commercial brands such as Crisco vegetable shortening can work too. Start out by working with what's easily available to you, then seek out different brands to experiment with new flavors!

YOGURT

Some yogurts are better than others, some yogurts are better than others—some yogurts' mothers are better than other yogurt's mothers . . . Here in Vancouver, we have the delightful plant-based Yoggu! brand; in the US, Anita's Yogurt is amazing. Find and test your favorite local or national brand of plant-based yogurt for the tangiest, creamiest one you can find, for making tangy cream cheese–like frostings.

REPLACING OUR OLD FRIEND, EGGHEAD

Eggs! Wow, did they ever become an intrinsic part of being alive, eh? Eggs for breakfast, eggs in cookies and cakes, eggs cracked into a blender for a Rocky-style smoothie!? Eggs give cakes structure and leavening, and help bind ingredients together. But guess what, fellow bakers? Eggs are replaceable! And you can leave them out altogether in many instances. Neat!

When I first started dabbling in plant-based cake baking twenty years ago, the most common way to replace eggs in a cake recipe was either with powdered egg replacer mixed with water or by making a gooey, thickened egg-substitute from soaked flax seeds. I've since found other methods that I enjoy using rather than egg replacer (which, depending on the brand, can sometimes give a gummy, over-thickened texture to cake batters), and the recipes in *Plantcakes* use either aquafaba or the chemical reaction of vinegar and baking soda to give structure and lift to the cakes.

VINEGAR AND BAKING SODA

I first learned about using vinegar and baking soda to help leaven a cake through the cookbook *How It All Vegan!* During the Great Depression in the early 1930s, eggs and butter were scarce and unaffordable, so brilliant home cooks relied on the chemical reaction between vinegar and baking soda to add bubbles and lift to their cakes. SCIENCE! Essentially, you combine your favorite plant milk with vinegar to make a buttermilk. This, together with baking soda in the dry ingredients, will create this magic cake-raising effect.

AQUAFABA

And then there's aquafaba! A.K.A. the liquid from a can of chickpeas. Isn't aquafaba a fun and fancy way of saying bean water? Whether you call it AF or BW, we can all agree that aquafaba is really a magical innovation for replacing eggs in plant-based baking. I was hesitant and skeptical when I first heard about it. How does it work? Would my baking taste beany? Could I make meringues, or even macarons with it? The answer is yes we sure can make incredibly delicious things with it, and no, it miraculously doesn't taste beany! It's pretty amazing stuff. It can also add structure via its delightful BEANY PROTEIN POWER to your cakes.

PREPARING AQUAFABA FOR BAKING: Strain the liquid from a can of unsalted chickpeas (also known as garbanzo beans) into a bowl. Reserve the chickpeas for another use, and store the aquafaba, covered, in the fridge until ready to use (it will keep for up to two days). You can freeze it too, for up to one month; once thawed, it will act just like its fresh counterpart.

NOTE: Note that 3 tbsp of aquafaba is the equivalent of one large egg.

USING AQUAFABA: When using aquafaba in a cake recipe, I give it a whisk first to froth and volumize it before adding it to the other ingredients. Aquafaba also whips up into a fluffy white meringue that can be piped and baked into sweet, crispy meringue kisses, or folded into finely ground almond flour for macarons, or used for meringue buttercreams (read much more about that on page 129).

VERSAWHIP

This is a more recent discovery of mine. Versawhip is a miracle soy-based powder that can be mixed with water to whip up into a fluffy meringue, for meringue-based buttercreams (see page 130) or in meringue cakes and decorations, such as the Mocha Dacquoise Cake (page 164), or the meringue mushrooms for Holiday Vibes Chocolate Stump Cake (page 155). Versawhip isn't as readily available as aquafaba, and can be pricier, but it's a fun product to try. Read more about preparing Versawhip on page 121.

OTHER OPTIONS

For baking beyond the recipes in this book, here are some other egg replacement options you can consider for your plant-based baking too.

APPLESAUCE: The pectin in applesauce acts as a binder for cake batter and will also add moisture without over-sweetening. Choose unsweetened applesauce when purchasing.

BANANAS: Beautiful, speckly, super ripe bananas—no other binding agents are needed when making banana cake, banana bread, or banana cupcakes. The ideal banana for baking has blackened skin and is ultra-ripe. The banana flesh may even just be a goopy mess, which to me is perfect! Haha. Embrace the fruit fly and let those bananas over-ripen.

FLAX: Soak ground flax seeds and you get a thick, viscous liquid that mimics the binding properties of an egg! One tbsp of flax seeds soaked in 3 tbsp of water equals one egg.

STORE-BOUGHT EGG REPLACER: Egg replacer contains thickening agents, such as potato starch, tapioca flour, and cellulose gum (made from the cell walls of plants!). Not all store-bought egg replacers are created equal, so you may have to find the one you like best. Some thicken up immediately into a gummy batter, while others simply help by giving a leavening boost.

COOL TOOLS

These are my favorite go-to tools for baking! Plus, my favorite tools to help you trim, fill, frost, and decorate your cake.

FOR BAKING

CAKE PANS: In *Plantcakes*, I use straight-sided 7- × 2-inch round or 8- × 2-inch round cake pans for my layer cakes. My go-tos are Fat Daddio's anodized aluminum pans, as they've lasted me for years already.

CANDY THERMOMETER: A candy thermometer or digital-read thermometer is super handy for making caramel, toffee, or brittle, such as the Caramel Almond Brittle (page 73), as well as the syrup for the Italian meringue buttercreams (pages 135–137).

DRY MEASURING CUPS AND SPOONS: Crucial taunt! I've had the same set of stainless-steel heavy-duty measuring cups and nested spoons for 15 years. Invest in a great-quality set, and you'll never have to buy them again.

KITCHEN SCALE: A scale is fun! Measuring exact ingredients is fun! But for real, it's satisfying to be exact, plus you can finally crack open all those UK cookbooks you've hoarded but never used because you didn't have a kitchen scale.

LIQUID MEASURING CUPS: The perfect vessel for whisking together a buttermilk, or for measuring vegetable oil or aquafaba. I like to have a few sizes on hand.

PARCHMENT PAPER: PP! Where would I be without you? I use parchment paper to create circles to line my cake pans with, to keep the cakes from sticking when I try to remove them. There are compostable brands of parchment paper, so I encourage you to use those!

RUBBER SPATULAS: I have probably fourteen spatulas in a range of sizes and cute colors, because I am a spatula nut. They have SO many uses, from hand-mixing final turns of a cake batter to scraping batter into cake pans.

SERRATED KNIFE: A long serrated bread knife is great for leveling the dome of cake layers. I generally try to avoid slicing single layers in two out of sheer paranoia of a lopsided cake, but this is a great tool for that too if you need to!

WHISKS: I love a whisking situation! I have a larger balloon whisk that I use all the time, as well as a small whisk for smaller jobs like whisking together dry ingredients, combining soy milk and vinegar to make a buttermilk, or gently bringing together a glossy chocolate ganache.

FOR DECORATING

CAKE BOARDS: Back in the day I would cover my own cake boards with cutely printed craft paper, but nowadays cake boards come in so many cool patterns and colors that I don't have to! Take your pick: marbled patterns, hot pink, turquoise, or plain old white is perfect too. (Hot tip: I reuse my cake boards for multiple cakes. To reuse, carefully wash the top with hot soapy water, avoiding getting the bottom cardboard damp, and dry completely before reusing.)

CAKE TURNTABLE: You can go big or go small with this purchase, but if you're planning to make plenty of cakes in the future, a turntable is a great investment! Plus, it will make you feel like you work in a fancy bakery. Most commonly, cake turntables are plastic or aluminum—I got my heavy-duty one with a 50% off coupon from a certain craft megastore several years ago.

OFFSET SPATULA: I feel truly naked without my collection of small offset spatulas. They have been with me through thick (frosting) and thin. I use them to spread frosting on cake layers, to frost the entire exterior of the cake, and even to gently reshape hot malleable cookies straight out of the oven back into a circle (because I deeply enjoy a nicely round cookie).

PIPING BAGS: You'll need a piping bag to make a jam dam for your cake fillings (see page 19) and, of course, for making frosting decorations like drop stars, rosettes, leaves, and swag! Piping bags are also crucial for meringue kisses and meringue mushrooms. I use 12- or 18-inch plastic disposable piping bags, but I wash them with hot and soapy water and reuse them again and again.

PIPING TIPS: These are the metal doohickeys that you plop into your piping bag to create magical fancy-looking shapes when you squeeze the frosting through. My personal favorite piping tips are Wilton 1M (for the classic cupcake frosting swirl), and 234 (its large multi-opening tip was originally meant for a grass effect, but I use it to pipe "animal fur"!). I have hundreds of piping tips in all shapes and sizes. But if you only get a few, I'd say Wilton's 1M, 4B, a large open circle tip, and a leaf tip would be fun ones to have in your arsenal. Here are the tips you'll find referenced in the recipes in this book:

- **Wilton 1M:** The classic "cupcake swirl" open star tip. This makes large rosettes, perfectly ruffly borders, drop stars, and meringue kisses. This tip is your piping-tip workhorse, and there's a reason I have 13 or so of them!

- **Wilton 4B:** Open star tip, and a true multi-pronged delight. The more prongs, the more ridges you can create in your frosting drop stars (to me, these drop stars have a 1980s vibe that I quite enjoy). Multi-pronged tips come in all sorts of sizes too, so you can make tinier drop stars or even cute little rosettes.

- **Large open circle tip:** Perfect for dollops of frosting that look like Hershey's kisses.

- **Small open circle tips:** Often used for writing on cakes. I have a helpful hint for that: gently drag a toothpick through the frosting on your chilled cake and write out your cake message first, then use that as a guide to follow with the piped frosting.

- **Multi-opening tip:** Also known as the grass tip. Great for piping furry-face cakes, one of my personal specialties, hehe. Check out cococakeland.com or @cococakeland on Instagram for a whole plethora of hairy frosting piped cakes.

- **Leaf tip:** Not only great for piping, uh, leaves, but I also use this as my special filler tip to fill in any gaps in the frosting on buttercream flower cakes (like the one on page 182). It can also be used to make a beautiful ruffle, perfect for cakes such as Dance Like No One Is Watching Earl Grey Cake (page 151), or those on pages 112 and 149 or any vintage-style cake.

STORING LEFTOVER CAKE

I have become somewhat of an expert on storing leftover cake, since I am always testing, baking, and photographing cakes. If you *happen* to find yourself with leftover cake, the best thing to do besides eat it is . . . gift it! Neighbors, friends, family, I'm sure they will all be very happy recipients! But if you want to store leftover cake, you can cut the cake up into individual slices and stack them in an airtight container with pieces of parchment paper between each slice (so the frosting doesn't get all mucked up). You can also freeze cake slices this way for up to a month (probably longer, but will it really last that long before someone eats it?!). Either way, bring the cake to room temperature before eating it (or eat it straight from the fridge, if you like cold cake, as I do!).

HOT TIPS

Here are the key baking hacks and helpful hints I've collected over the years. Before you begin any recipe, a great rule for all cookbooks is to read through the recipe from start to finish before jumping in. That way you'll have a general idea of what you're in for, and of course can ensure you have all the ingredients in your kitchen before you begin. Prepping your ingredients and measuring them out beforehand into little bowls can also minimize "oh shnikey, did I forget to add the salt?" moments.

BAKE WITH A SCALE

For many years, I baked using volume measurements only, putting my trust in measuring cups and spoons. While this has always worked out for me, there's also something very satisfying about being precise. Investing in a small kitchen scale (you can get them for around $20) will give you exact results each time. For the recipes in this book, I've included weight in both US cups and grams for those of you who enjoy using a food scale and measuring ingredients by weight!

PREP YOUR PANS

Spray the base and interior sides of your cake pans with vegetable oil or nonstick cooking spray, then line them with parchment paper cut to size. I know we've all seen too many episodes of *Nailed It!* where the cake gets stuck in the pan at crunch time, and we really don't want to be that person.

KEEP AN EAGLE EYE ON YOUR CAKES WHILE THEY'RE BAKING

All ovens run differently, so look for visual clues that the cake is done—for instance, a light golden brown color for vanilla cakes, a slight doming of the cake for chocolate cakes—rather than just going by the baking time given in the recipe. Don't forget to trust your nose. If you start smelling cake, your cake may be done very soon, if it's not already! I start testing my cake for doneness up to 3 minutes before the suggested baking time given in a recipe by inserting a toothpick in the center of the cake. If it comes out with only moist crumbs gently clinging to it, it's time to take the cake out. If it comes out with slightly wet batter on it, keep baking and checking in two- to three-minute increments until it's ready. If it comes out completely dry . . . it's time to soak those dry layers with syrup! (See page 16.)

STAY COOL

Once the cakes are baked, I set my cake pans on wire racks to let the cakes cool completely in their pans. Let your cakes *fully* cool before frosting—melted, runny frosting caused by a too-hot cake is right up there in sadness levels with dropping an ice cream cone on the sidewalk or a bird pooping on your sandwich at the beach. (That has never happened to me, but I have been pooped on by birds three times in ONE DAY.)

POWER-CHILL YOUR CAKES

I do this often when I'm in a time crunch to start frosting—pop the cakes, still in their pans, in the freezer and chill for 20 to 30 minutes to take the hot edge off.

EXPLORE SYRUPS AND SOAKS

Moistening cake layers with syrups and soaks is a juiced-up trick of the cake trade. Not only does it provide insurance that your cake will stay moist, particularly when you bake a cake in advance, but soaks such as coffee syrup, lemon syrup, vanilla milk, banana milk, or milk tea can infuse cake layers with even more flavor.

IF IN DOUBT, CHILL AGAIN

If you enjoy being super picky about the visual appearance of cake slices, may I suggest refrigerating the cake for an hour before slicing? You will get cleaner slices if the cake is cold and you use a sharp (not serrated) knife. And here's an extra pro tip: heat your knife under hot water, and dry it with a towel before slicing for an extra-clean cut, and always wipe the knife clean between slices too.

CAKE SCRAPS ARE COOL TOO!

Never scrap your cake scraps! Instead, try taking scraps (or any leftover cupcakes or cakes cut into smaller pieces) and layering them in empty jam jars with extra frostings, syrups, soaks, or any textural elements you have on hand. I like to place a dollop of frosting in the bottom of the jar first, and then add a few pieces of cake and squish it all down so the frosting fills the jar's bottom. Add some syrup, more frosting, some berries or leftover toffee bits, then another few pieces of cake, and keep building from there! It's the perfect way to use up any of the yummy cake elements you've prepared, and you can share these jars of love with neighbors, family, and friends. Cake scraps are also delicious transformed into a trifle with coconut whip or yogurt, and fresh or frozen fruit—which makes for a decadent leftover cake breakfast.

(Of course, cake scraps can also be jammed directly into your mouth in a delicious emotional eating frenzy right after trimming your cakes.)

HOW TO FILL + FROST A CAKE

If you're like me, then you have very likely made a real ugly duckling of a cake in your past—because *who knew* about things like leveling your cake to make flat cake layers, or starting with a crumb-coat frosting to lock crumbs in a crumb-prison, or using piping bags to make things look fancy? Well, we do now! And below I outline every step of how to fill and frost a cake. In these steps I lay it all out for a three-layer cake, but you can easily adapt this to frost a two-layer cake or even a single-layer cake.

Don't fret if your first few attempts at frosting still don't look like all the pretty cakes on your dang social media. Like almost any skill, you may flop at it first before you get good! Keep on keeping on, and with each cake, your frosting and decorating will just keep getting better.

GET EVERYTHING READY
Bake and completely cool your cakes. Make your buttercream and/or any other frostings or fillings, and any syrups or soaks (if using). Then get your cake board or plate ready, and your cake turntable, if you have one. Place a small dollop of frosting on the cake board (this is to help secure the cake to the board, to stop it from moving around when you are frosting).

PREPARE THE CAKES
Carefully run a small offset spatula around the edges of the first pan to loosen the cake. Turn out this first cake layer, remove the parchment paper from the bottom, and then place the cake board over the flat bottom of the cake. Quickly but carefully flip the cake and board back over, so the cake is now right side up, sitting on the cake board.

Using a serrated bread knife, carefully saw off any baked-up dome on the top of the cake, leveling the top of the cake so it's flat. (Don't toss the trimmings though—save them for snacks—page 16!) Now place the cake board onto your cake turntable, if using.

FILL THE FIRST LAYER
If the recipe calls for a syrup or soak, start with that. Using a pastry brush, brush a generous but not too wild amount of syrup or soak on the top of the first layer of cake.

If you are using jam, that goes on next. Place a dollop of jam in the center of the top of the cake and, using an offset spatula, spread it out, stopping about a quarter of an inch from the edge of the cake. Or, if you are using just frosting, dollop a large plop into the center of the top of the cake. (You can also use a retractable ice cream scoop to get the exact same amount of frosting between each layer.) Using an offset spatula, spread the frosting almost to the edge of the cake, but not all the way to the very edge—you don't want the frosting to smoosh out the sides once you put the next cake layer on top—and gently press down to make the layers stick together.

TRY THE JAM DAM METHOD...
If you want to add a more generous amount of filling to your layers (be it jam or chocolate ganache) but still keep it from smooshing out the sides, use one of two methods.

The first is to create a "dam" to prevent any filling from escaping by piping buttercream around the edge of each layer of cake (known as the "jam dam"). To do this, fit your piping bag with a large open circle tip and fill the bag with buttercream.

Pipe a generous border of buttercream around the edge of the cake layer. Then add your filling (whatever it may be) inside the walls of the dam (photo 1)—but be careful not to overfill, as it can goop over the sides of the dam.

. . . OR DUGOUT POOL METHOD

The other technique for adding extra filling is the "dugout pool." For this method, first add a thick layer of buttercream on top of the first layer of cake. Next, using your offset spatula, dig out some of the buttercream from the center—to create a divot or a pool in the buttercream that can then be filled—leaving about a one-inch border of buttercream around the cake. Fill the pool with your chosen filling.

ADD AND FILL THE SECOND CAKE LAYER

Turn the next layer of cake out onto a flat surface (I find the flat underside of the pan the cake was baked in very handy for this) and level the top of the cake with the serrated knife.

Carefully place the next cake layer cut side down on top of the filling of the first layer. Repeat the syrup or soak step, and the jam and frosting steps for the second layer, as required for the recipe.

TOP WITH THE THIRD CAKE LAYER

With the final cake layer, repeat the leveling step above, then carefully place the third layer cut side down on top of the top layer of buttercream, leaving the top of your cake as level as possible. If you are using a syrup or soak, add a final soaking now to the top of the cake. Give your cake a few turns to look everything over, and adjust the layers slightly as needed to make sure everything looks fairly straight and level before you begin frosting (photo 2).

APPLY THE CRUMB COAT

Place a large dollop of buttercream on top of the cake. Using an offset spatula, spread the buttercream evenly over the top layer, then work your way down the sides of the cake, covering every surface of the cake with buttercream (photo 3).

Using a cake bench scraper, smooth out the sides and top of the cake and add more buttercream to fill in any holes. A lip of buttercream may form at the top edge of the cake. To counter this, use your offset spatula to pull the buttercream inward toward the center of the top layer, smoothing as you go (photo 4).

CHILL THE CAKE

Chill the cake in your fridge or freezer to set it. I do either a twelve-minute power chill in the freezer, or a thirty-minute "I have a bit more time" chill in the fridge—and I always set the timer so I don't forget about my cake. (Note: This is probably my cake paranoia talking, but make sure you don't have anything glaringly strong-smelling in your fridge, as your gentle buttercream cake friend might absorb the smell—onions, garlic, etc. begone!)

CRUMB COAT

What is a crumb coat, you ask? It's the first layer of frosting you apply to your cake to lock in all the crumbs that might get pulled off the cake while you're frosting. It also gives your second, final, coat something to stick to. The key is to chill your cake in the fridge or freezer after you have applied the crumb coat to re-harden the buttercream. That way, when you frost the next layer, the crumbs won't infiltrate the buttercream, and you'll get a more professional-looking cake as a result.

APPLY THE SECOND LAYER OF FROSTING

Bring your chilled cake out of the fridge or freezer and place it back on your cake turntable. Apply another large dollop of buttercream to the top of the cake, again using your offset spatula, and spread it over the top and sides (photo 5). For this second layer of frosting, there are three main styles of frosting finish you can choose from:

AU NATUREL: If you are going for a swoopy, more natural look for your finished cakes, use your offset spatula to create swoop designs in the frosting (photo 6). Finish the cake with fresh fruit or edible flowers for a colorful "au naturel" look!

SMOOTH: If you want a smooth cake, use your cake bench scraper to carefully smooth the sides and top of the cake after you have applied the buttercream, and use your offset spatula to smooth the top lip edge of buttercream back up and over onto the top of the cake (photos 7 + 8). Add buttercream borders and drop stars, if desired.

NAKED: Or Nudi-T, as we call it in our household. If you want a naked cake, stop frosting at the crumb-coat stage, then use your cake bench scraper to scrape away the buttercream from the sides of the cake. The buttercream will remain intact on top of the cake and in between the cake layers, but scraping it away from the sides adds a nice striped effect to the cake, with the cake layers and buttercream layers in view (photos 9 + 10). (Save the scraped-away buttercream to use with your cake scraps in a jar trifles—see page 16.)

Once you are happy with your cake, use a paper towel to carefully wipe up any extra buttercream on your cake board.

FINAL FROST STAGE

Congratulations, you've now reached the final frost stage! The next step is to add all the decorative frosting elements that you like—maybe a piped shell border or some drop stars, for example—and then the decorations, like sprinkles, fresh berries, herbs, and flowers.

PUT IT IN YOUR BAG + PIPE IT

Hashtag creation is a terrible art form, and sometimes I am an idiot who likes to come up with them. Will hashtags cease to exist one day? #Idontknow. My favorite hashtag I've come up with is the very silly #putitinyourbagandpipeit because . . . marijuana is funny? Dad jokes are cool? Back when I was first learning about cake decorating, I had a total light bulb moment with piping bags. So *that's* how they get things to look all neat and tidy and ruffly! You force-jam some frosting into a baggie fitted with a specially shaped nozzle, and as you squeeze, cool shapes come out! The piping bag has been the savior of many cake decorators, covering wonkily frosted cake edges and borders the world over.

The piping bag will be your best friend, should you want it to be. It can help take your cakes from "Hey look, a sixteen-month-old-baby made that cake!" to "Ooh, I believe a human person older than a baby made that cake." You might even get to "Hey, do you work at the supermarket bakery power-piping sheet cakes?" level. Follow the steps below, and who knows how far you'll go!

PREPARING YOUR PIPING BAG

Piping bags come in a few different sizes, the most common being twelve inches—this size will fit your typical piping tips and couplers, if using. If you have a big piping job ahead of you, you can use an eighteen-inch bag. I use clear plastic disposable bags, but I reuse them by washing them out with hot soapy water, then rinsing and letting them dry.

If you are using a plastic piping bag, snip off the tip with sharp scissors. If you plan to use different piping tips with the same color buttercream, you can use a coupler with your bag, allowing you to swap out piping tips and use the same piping bag for different piping techniques. Couplers have two components: the first is the piece you place inside the piping bag, which your piping tip then nestles on top of. The second is the ring that screws the tip in place on the outside of the bag. Personally, I usually forgo the coupler all together and just pull the piping tip snugly into place.

FILLING YOUR PIPING BAG

To fill the piping bag, I use a tall plastic deli container or large glass to assist. Place the piping bag inside the vessel, pulling its edges over the sides of the container to create a nice opening. Then, using a spatula, fill the bag about two-thirds full of buttercream. Lift the bag out of the container, twist the end closed, and squeeze the bag so the buttercream flows into the tip.

PIPE DREAMS

Now that you've put it in your bag—it's time to pipe it! If you like, you can practice piping styles on parchment paper or a plate first. Then you can scrape the buttercream back into the bowl or piping bag to use after you've practiced. In the recipes, you'll see I mention a few different piping styles, and on the following pages you'll find the how-to on the styles used most often in this book.

BORDERS

DOLLOPS

DROP STARS

ROSETTES

RUFFLES

SWAG

BORDERS: Using a piping tip fitted with an open star tip such as a Wilton 1M or 4B, you can create cute shell borders on your cakes (this is shown in the photo opposite using a 1M tip, and on page 30 in peach on the bottom row, also using a 1M tip, and in turquoise on the second bottom row, using a 4B tip). Hold the piping bag with your dominant hand at a 45-degree angle to the top edge of the cake. Squeeze the piping bag with medium pressure so that a ridged buttercream ball shape forms, then pull gently away, creating a little tail. Pipe the next shell on top of the tail, and then repeat this pattern until you've piped the entire border. You can do the top edge border and the bottom border too. You can also create a ruffle effect border using your leaf tip, such as Wilton 70 (shown in pink on the 5th row on page 30).

DOLLOPS: I also call these "blobettes" (a potential new band name?). They're a Hershey's Kiss–like shape as you see pictured opposite. Using a piping bag fitted with an open circle tip, hold the piping bag upright at a 90-degree angle against the cake surface. Squeeze the piping bag so a blob of buttercream comes out, then pull directly up to create the "point."

DROP STARS: Using a piping bag fitted with an open star tip such as a Wilton 1M or 4B, hold the piping bag with your dominant hand at a 90-degree angle against the cake surface. Squeeze the piping bag with medium pressure. As a drop star forms, pull upward to release. (Drop stars are shown in the photo opposite using a Wilton 1M tip, and on page 30 in purple in the second row, also using a 1M tip, and in yellow in the third row, using a 4B tip.)

ROSETTES: These are cute, easy piped roses! Using a piping tip fitted with an open star tip (shown opposite using a Wilton 8B tip and in the top row on page 30 in peach and purple using a 1M tip, and in turquoise and yellow using a 4B tip), hold the piping bag with

PUT IT IN YOUR BAG + PIPE IT **27**

your dominant hand and position the bag on the cake where you would like the center of the rose to be. Squeeze the piping bag in a counterclockwise motion in one rotation, pulling upward to release.

RUFFLES: I love the ruffly look so much! Using a piping bag fitted with a leaf tip (such as the Wilton 70, as shown in the photo on page 27 and in pink on page 30), hold the piping bag at a 90-degree angle to the cake surface. Squeeze the piping bag and pipe ruffles in a back and forth motion, piping the next ruffle on top of the tail of the last ruffle, back toward yourself. This one may take a few rounds of practice, but once you get the pattern you'll be all set!

SWAG: To pipe swag, you're going to be piping ruffly waves in an upside-down rainbow or "V" shape (as shown in the photo on page 27), using a piping bag fitted with a Wilton 70 tip. To be exact, you can measure and mark your swag start and end points first before you begin piping. To do this, cut a piece of parchment paper to the size of your cake, fold it in half, then in half again (and again a third time if you would like more swag!) to create equal sections. Unfold it and place it gently on top of your cake, then, using a toothpick, mark the cake where each swag will begin and end.

Hold the piping bag so the wide end of the tip is against the cake at a 45-degree angle. Pipe and wiggle the bag to create ruffly waves that touch the cake in an upside-down rainbow shape, starting from the first mark and finishing the swag at the next mark. Repeat until the cake is all swagged out! You can do another string of swag underneath the first, if desired.

BAKING WITH KIDS

My son, Teddy, is nine years old at the time I'm writing this, and over the years, we've spent more and more time baking together. It's just such an amazing skill for a kid to learn, so I encourage you to bake with the kids in your life! Try not to blow your top too much in the kitchen (like I have in the past, haha), and let them have fun with it. You can clean up the flour tornado later.

FONDANT!

I've built part of my cake career making super cute animal cakes, so I wanted to include an option for you to turn *your* cakes into animals too—like this blue cat cake I made for Teddy's 9th birthday! The base of this kitty cake is the Vanilla Cake (page 63) filled and frosted to the final frost stage (pages 19–22), with Vanilla Swiss Meringue Buttercream (page 130) tinted with a tiny amount of blue gel color. The ears, facial features, and whiskers are made of vegan-friendly, store-bought fondant (I like Satin Ice brand)!

Working with fondant is very similar to working with Play-Do, hehe. To make this kitty's features, I shaped the blue fondant into thick, triangular, ear-shaped pieces, and cut out smaller pink-colored inner ears. I adhered the pink inner ears to the blue ears using a tiny, toothpick-tip amount of water. Then, to anchor the ears to the cake, I used a wooden BBQ skewer cut in two, one piece each for each ear.

I shaped the whiskers, tiny nose, and mouth by hand. For the eyes and cheeks, I rolled out the fondant using a rolling pin and cut the shapes using circle cookie cutters and the round edge of a piping tip, then pressed these pieces right into the buttercream. Done! Meow you've made a purr-fectly adorable kitty cake, hehe.

CUPCAKE DREAMS

Cupcakes bring childhood nostalgia to any party or event: individually wrapped, and often frosted with a cute buttercream swirl, they can be an easy way to cake it up, especially for kids' birthdays. Finish your cupcakes with sprinkles, or chocolate chips, or a halved strawberry—whatever floats your boat!

CLASSIC CUPCAKE SWIRL: Using a piping bag fitted with an open star tip, such as Wilton 1M or 4B, hold the piping bag upright at a 90-degree angle to the top the cupcake. Starting at the edge, squeeze the piping bag and begin piping the buttercream in a continuous circle; without releasing the piping bag, continue piping concentric circles until you reach the center of the cupcake—pulling upward to release.

CUPCAKE DROP STARS: Using a piping bag fitted with an open star tip, such as the Wilton 1M or 4B, hold the piping bag at a 90-degree angle to the top of the cupcake. Simply squeeze and pull upward to create each star shape (as shown in turquoise and fuchsia on the photo opposite).

CUPCAKE RUFFLES: Using a piping bag fitted with a petal tip (with the wider portion of the tip on the bottom), such as the Wilton 104, hold the piping bag at a 90-degree angle to the top of the cupcake. Squeeze the piping bag and allow buttercream to flow out while simultaneously moving your hand in a gentle zigzag motion to create a line of ruffles (as shown in yellow and grass green on the photo opposite). You can practice this on parchment paper first before your cupcake!

AU NATUREL: No piping tips? No problem. For a more rustic and natural look, use an offset spatula to add a generous dollop of buttercream to the top of your cupcake. Use the offset spatula to spread the buttercream outward to the edges.

GARDEN PARTY VANILLA LEMON CUPCAKES
(PAGE 210)

FINISHING TOUCHES . . .

CRUNCHY, CRUMBLY, CRISPY COOL
I love alliteration just as much as I love a textural element when it comes to building and finishing my cakes, whether it be freeze-dried strawberries, classic rainbow sprinkles, or homemade toffee bits. My ideal cake has soft cake layers, creamy frosting, some sort of tangy juicy aspect (from a syrup or soak, or fresh fruit, for example) and a crunchy sweet and salty texture to finish. Here are some of my favorite textural accoutrements that can be sprinkled liberally onto your cakes. Add these just before serving (so the frosting doesn't soften the crunch into a non-crunch).

BIRTHDAY CAKE CRUMBLES (PAGE 91): Inspired by Milk Bar, these are like birthday cake–flavored cookie crumbles with rainbow sprinkles.

CANDIED HAZELNUTS (PAGE 115): Addictive, and sweet and salty, these add a toasty candied crunch as well as some striking visual decor when broken into shards.

CARAMEL ALMOND BRITTLE (PAGE 73): I love the crunch of a toasted almond, chopped up into caramel brittle, adding texture and salty-sweet crunch to cakes.

FLAKY SEA SALT: Perfect on top of rich chocolate ganache or sweet frosting to balance the flavor and give texture.

FREEZE-DRIED STRAWBERRIES OR RASPBERRIES: Crisp, and full of deep flavor and tang. These can be found at select grocery stores (such as Trader Joe's) and readily online.

MERINGUE KISSES (PAGE 177): Crispy sweet meringues that can be used to decorate as they are or crushed up and sprinkled on top! Meringue loses some of its crispness when moistened by frosting, so I try to add it just before serving.

OATMEAL COOKIE CRUMBLES (PAGE 83): Sweet and salty crispy oatmeal cookie crunch = very addictive. Leftovers can be sprinkled on your morning yogurt parfait or as an after-dinner treat on ice cream and frozen fruit.

PEANUT BUTTER CUP CRUNCH (PAGE 107): If you love peanut butter cups, you'll love this crunch (pictured opposite); it's essentially PB cups chopped up and ready to sprinkle.

SPRINKLES: Rainbow sprinkles are the finishing touch to so many cakes and cupcakes! Kids love 'em, adults love 'em, and you can find vegan and naturally colored ones through my cake pal Rosie at Sweetapolita! (See Resources, page 225.)

STREUSEL (PAGE 55): Dreamy crumble topping that gives sweet and salty deliciousness to sour cream cakes, breakfast cakes, pies, and muffins.

TOASTED COCONUT (PAGE 187): A tropical, textured flavor blast—I love the smell of toasted coconut baking in the oven. Leftovers can be added to granola!

TOFFEE CRUNCH (PAGE 85): Buttery, crunchy toffee bits are one of my favorite additions to cakes, both sprinkled between cake layers and as another sprinkle on top to finish.

FRUIT + FLOWERS

As a general rule, when working with fruit for a cake (such as citrus for zests and syrups, or berries for making jam or decorating), I try to choose organic, local, and in-season fruit when possible. Flowers should be organic, certified edible, and unsprayed. Edible flowers can be found at the farmers' market, or at large organic foods chains in the herbs section—or you could always grow them yourself! I am an absolutely horrific gardener, but even I have managed to grow bachelor's buttons, marigolds, and violets in pots, all from seed!

CANDIED FRUIT: Adorning a cake with candied citrus peels adds texture, sweet-bitter complexity, and color! You can use it to decorate any citrusy-themed cakes any time you want, to add a sprinkle of complex flavor.

EDIBLE FRESH FLOWERS: Edible flowers add such a pretty pop of color and a natural-feeling vibe to so many cakes. Adding flowers is an easy way to make a simple cake look extra special.

EDIBLE PRESSED DRIED FLOWERS: Pressed and dried flowers look so pretty on cakes! Plan to start two weeks in advance so your flowers have time to dry out and flatten. To dry your fresh flowers, lay them on a piece of plain white paper. Place another piece of paper on top of that, then squash it with a big old book to flatten. That's it! Just allow them to flatten for two weeks to fully dry out.

Citrus fruits of your choice (lemons, oranges, or grapefruits)

1 cup (200g) granulated white sugar

1 cup (250ml) water

EASY CANDIED CITRUS

This recipe is very loosey-goosey. The main principles are: blanch your citrus peels to soften them and remove a little bitterness, saturate them in simple syrup, then add texture and even more sweetness by rolling 'em around in granulated white sugar.

Using a sharp paring knife, cut away the outermost peel from your citrus fruit, then slice the peel lengthwise into thin strips. Save the cut fruit for another use.

In a medium saucepan set over medium-high heat, add the citrus peels, sugar, and water and cook until the peels are tender, about 15 minutes. Using a slotted spoon, transfer the peels to a wire rack to dry, discarding the blanching water.

Using the same saucepan, bring the sugar and water to a boil, dissolving the sugar in the water to create a simple syrup. Add the peels back to the pan and boil the syrup until it reduces and thickens to half the amount, and the peels soften further and turn translucent.

Remove the peels from the pan and let them dry for about an hour on a wire rack. Reserve the citrusy simple syrup for cake soaks or for jazzing up your bubbly water or cocktails. Store the syrup in a covered jar in the fridge for up to 1 month.

Once the peels are dry, toss with more sugar to coat. Store the candied fruit in an airtight container in a cool, dry place for up to 1 month.

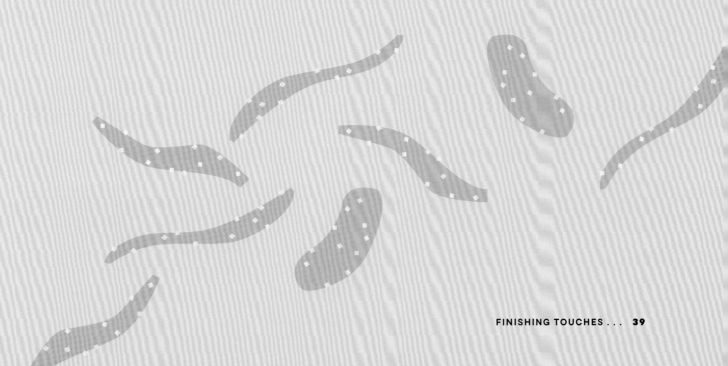

FINISHING TOUCHES . . . 39

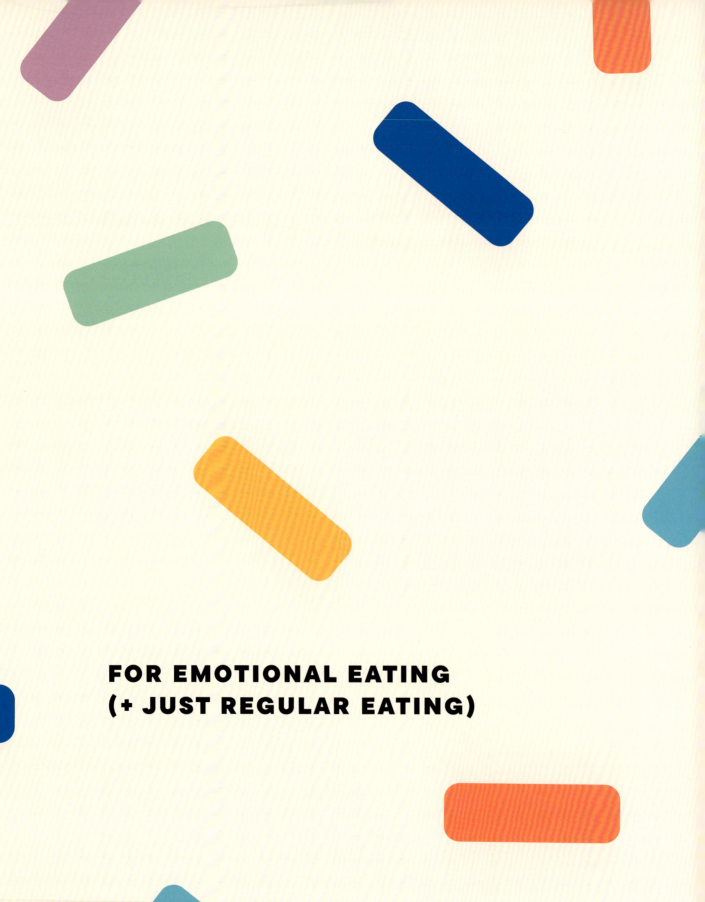

**FOR EMOTIONAL EATING
(+ JUST REGULAR EATING)**

1

SNACKING CAKES

Apple Olive Oil Cake

1½ cups (210g) all-purpose flour

1¼ tsp baking powder

1 tsp fine sea salt

¾ tsp cinnamon

¾ cup (150g) brown sugar

½ cup (125ml) olive oil

¼ cup (70ml) unsweetened applesauce

1 tbsp pure vanilla extract

3 medium organic apples such as Honeycrisp

Frosting

1 recipe Maple Cream Cheese Frosting (page 140)

Flaky sea salt (optional)

APPLE OLIVE OIL CAKE WITH MAPLE CREAM CHEESE FROSTING

MAKES ONE 9-INCH SINGLE-LAYER CAKE

If this cake was a movie, I would call it *Autumn's Bounty: The Snacking Cake*. The stars of this movie are the toasty fall flavors—featuring baked apple, cinnamon, brown sugar, and maple syrup—presented in a round snacking cake perfect for afternoon tea. My favorite apples to use for this are the aptly named Honeycrisp—they're sweet but with body that can hold up well in the oven—but feel free to choose your favorite firm-fleshed apple or combination of apples instead. Go for a fruity, high-quality olive oil and you'll taste the difference, and spring for that bottle of pure maple syrup while you're at it too. The cake is inspired by Yotam Ottolenghi's version, but veganized, of course! And feel free to omit the frosting—the cake on its own is delicious and can be sliced up for a tidy little lunchbox treat.

MAKE THE CAKE

Preheat the oven to 350°F (175°C). Prepare a 9- × 2-inch round cake pan by spritzing it with vegetable oil and lining with a parchment paper circle cut to size, and then spritzing again with oil, to prevent sticking.

In a medium bowl, whisk together the flour, baking powder, salt, and cinnamon.

In the bowl of a stand mixer fitted with the paddle attachment, mix the brown sugar, olive oil, applesauce, and vanilla extract on low speed until combined. Add the dry ingredients, pulse to combine, then mix on low speed until incorporated, about 30 seconds.

Peel and core the apples, then dice into 1-inch pieces (you're looking for 2 cups/260g diced apple in total). Add the apples to the stand mixer and pulse to combine. The batter will be on the thicker side.

BAKE THE CAKE

Pour the batter into the prepared cake pan, using an offset spatula to spread it in the pan and level it. Give the pan a light tap on the counter to reduce any air bubbles. Bake for 40–45 minutes, until the cake edges and top are browned, and a toothpick inserted into the center comes out with only moist crumbs.

Let the cake cool completely in its pan set on top of a wire rack.

ASSEMBLE THE CAKE

Remove the cooled cake from the pan. Dollop a generous amount of the maple cream cheese frosting onto the center of the cake. Using an offset spatula, spread the frosting to the edges of the cake. Finish with a pinch of flaky sea salt.

This cake will taste freshest eaten within a day of making it, but can be stored in the fridge, covered, for up to 3 days. See page 13 for storage notes.

Blackberry Maple Breakfast Cake

1 cup (250ml) soy milk

½ cup (125ml) pure maple syrup

¼ cup (60ml) vegetable oil

2 tsp apple cider vinegar

1 tsp pure vanilla extract

1 cup (140g) all-purpose flour

½ cup (75g) whole wheat flour

2 tsp baking powder

½ tsp baking soda

½ tsp cinnamon

½ tsp fine sea salt

1 cup (125g) fresh or frozen blackberries

2 tbsp turbinado or raw sugar

Maple Coconut Whipped Cream

2 cups (500ml) coconut cream, refrigerated in the cans for 24 hours

½ cup (65g) icing sugar, sifted

1 tbsp pure maple syrup

1 tsp pure vanilla extract

Pinch of salt

Topping

Pure maple syrup, for drizzling (optional)

Fresh blackberries (optional)

BLACKBERRY MAPLE BREAKFAST CAKE WITH MAPLE COCONUT WHIPPED CREAM

MAKES ONE 8-INCH SQUARE OR 9-INCH ROUND SINGLE-LAYER CAKE

As a parent, I'm always adding whole grain flour to my baked goods to get that fiber flowing—a happy kid is a kid with a productive digestive system, hehe. You won't notice the taste of the whole wheat flour in this recipe, though; it's all about the hints of cinnamon and maple syrup dotted with the tart-sweet burst of blackberries. This is a simple cake to start your mornings and much healthier than a bowl of sugary cereal—although, dolloped with cold, sweet maple coconut whipped cream and sprinkled with your favorite fruit, it will feel more like dessert!

MAKE THE CAKE

Preheat the oven to 350°F (175°C). Prepare an 8-inch square or 9- × 2-inch round cake pan by spritzing it with vegetable oil and lining with parchment paper cut to size, and then spritzing again with oil, to prevent sticking.

In the bowl of a stand mixer fitted with the paddle attachment, mix the soy milk, maple syrup, vegetable oil, apple cider vinegar, and vanilla extract on low speed until combined. Turn off the mixer.

In a large bowl, whisk together the all-purpose flour, whole wheat flour, baking powder, baking soda, cinnamon, and salt. Add the dry mixture to the stand mixer. Turn the mixer to low speed and mix to combine until a batter forms, about 30 seconds. Carefully fold in the blackberries, reserving a handful to dot the top of the batter.

BAKE THE CAKE

Pour the batter into the prepared cake pan, tapping the pan on the counter a few times to reduce any air bubbles. Nestle the reserved blackberries into the batter, then sprinkle evenly with the turbinado sugar. Bake for 26–30 minutes, until the cake edges are lightly browned, and a toothpick inserted into the center comes out with only moist crumbs.

continued

Let the cake cool completely in its pan set on top of a wire rack.

MAKE THE MAPLE COCONUT WHIPPED CREAM

Place the metal bowl and whisk attachment of your stand mixer or handheld mixer in the freezer to chill for 15–20 minutes.

Fit your stand mixer with the chilled bowl and whisk, and whip the coconut cream until thickened and fluffy. Add the icing sugar, maple syrup, vanilla extract, and pinch of salt and beat for another minute to combine. The maple coconut whipped cream can be stored in the fridge for up to 3 days.

ASSEMBLE THE CAKE

Remove the cooled cake from the pan. Slice into squares and dollop each slice with a generous amount of the maple coconut whipped cream. Drizzle with maple syrup, and top with fresh blackberries.

Store the whipped cream and cake separately, and slice and assemble as needed for serving. This cake will taste freshest eaten within a day of making it, but can be stored (before topping with whipped cream) in the fridge, covered, for up to 3 days. See page 13 for storage notes.

Chocolate Brownie Cake

1 cup (120g) extra-fine almond flour

½ cup (95g) potato starch

½ cup (60g) Dutch-process cocoa powder

¾ tsp fine sea salt

½ cup (125ml) soy milk

1 tsp instant coffee granules

¾ cup (185ml) full-fat coconut milk or coconut cream

1 cup (175g) callets or chopped pieces bittersweet or semisweet plant-based chocolate

1 cup (200g) granulated white sugar

1 tsp pure vanilla extract

Frosting

Raspberry jam (page 141) or use your favorite store-bought

½ recipe Vanilla Buttercream (page 125)

Fresh raspberries

CHOCOLATE ALMOND BROWNIE CAKE WITH VANILLA BUTTERCREAM

MAKES ONE 8-INCH SINGLE-LAYER CAKE   (GF)

I like to slather this rich gluten-free chocolate almond brownie cake with a raspberry jam that's hidden under its simple vanilla frosting. The pairing of chocolate and raspberry has a real "1980s cruise ship plated dessert" vibe, but I think I will always love this flavor combination! You can also swap out the vanilla frosting for Chocolate Ganache Frosting (page 139) or Chocolate Buttercream (page 125). The gluten-free chocolate cake part of this recipe is inspired by the delicious vegan blog Zardyplants.

MAKE THE CHOCOLATE BROWNIE CAKE

Preheat the oven to 350°F (175°C). Prepare an 8- × 2-inch round cake pan by spritzing it with vegetable oil and lining with a parchment paper circle cut to size, and then spritzing again with oil, to prevent sticking.

In a large bowl, whisk together the almond flour, potato starch, cocoa powder, and salt.

In a small bowl, combine the soy milk and instant coffee granules, stirring to dissolve.

In a medium saucepan set over medium-low heat, gently heat the coconut milk. Add the chocolate pieces and stir until the chocolate has melted. Stir in the sugar. Remove the saucepan from the heat and pour the chocolate into the bowl of a stand mixer fitted with the paddle attachment. With the mixer on low speed, add the soy milk-coffee mixture and vanilla extract, mixing until combined.

Turn the mixer off and carefully add the dry ingredients, pulsing to combine. Mix on low speed for another 15–30 seconds, scraping down the side of the bowl if needed, until a smooth batter forms.

BAKE THE CAKE

Pour the cake batter into the prepared cake pan. Give the pan a light tap on the counter to reduce any air bubbles. Bake for 35–40 minutes, until a toothpick inserted into the center comes out clean.

Let the cake cool completely in its pan set on a wire rack. Almond flour cakes can be fragile, so handle with care: when cooled completely, run an offset spatula around the edges of the cake to loosen it, then refrigerate, covered and still in its pan, for at least 1 hour and up to overnight.

continued

ASSEMBLE THE CAKE

Place a cake plate directly on top of the completely cooled cake in its pan, and do a very fast flip, turning the cake out so it is now on the plate. Remove the parchment paper from the cake.

Using an offset spatula, add a thin layer of raspberry jam to the top of the cake. Using a piping tip fitted with a large open star tip, pipe drop stars of buttercream on top, starting from the outside border and working your way inward in circles. Top with a single fresh raspberry for a Wayne Thiebaud feel, or decorate with many raspberries if you prefer!

This cake will taste freshest eaten within a day of making it, but can be stored in the fridge, covered, for up to 3 days. See page 13 for storage notes.

Lemon Cake

- 1 cup (200g) granulated white sugar + 2 heaping tbsp for sprinkling (optional)
- 2 tbsp lemon zest
- 1½ cups (210g) all-purpose flour
- 2 tsp baking powder
- ½ tsp fine sea salt
- ¾ cup (187g) plant-based sour cream
- 1 tbsp lemon juice
- ½ cup (112g) unsalted plant-based butter, melted
- ½ lemon, thinly sliced

Vanilla Bean Glaze

- 1 cup (130g) icing sugar, sifted + more as needed
- 2 tbsp soy milk + more as needed
- 1 tsp vanilla bean paste
- Pinch of fine sea salt
- Fresh raspberries (optional)
- Edible flowers (optional)

LEMON LOAF CAKE WITH VANILLA BEAN GLAZE

MAKES ONE 8-INCH SQUARE OR 9-INCH ROUND SINGLE-LAYER CAKE

Calling all lemon lovers! It's so satisfying to whip up this bright, tangy lemon-loaf-like snacking cake—it's instant cakey sunshine. Rubbing the lemon zest with sugar releases the lemon oil right into the sugar, giving the cake that extra bit of lemony brightness. I also like to add very thin slices of lemon to the top of the batter and then sprinkle the whole thing with sugar—it forms an almost candied-lemon top crust as it bakes. Then you drizzle the whole thing with a simple vanilla bean glaze (and if you don't have vanilla bean paste, simply add a teaspoon of pure vanilla extract in its place).

MAKE THE CAKE

Preheat the oven to 350°F (175°C). Prepare an 8-inch square or 9- × 2-inch round cake pan by spritzing it with vegetable oil and lining with parchment paper cut to size, and then spritzing again with oil, to prevent sticking.

In a small bowl, combine the sugar with the lemon zest, rubbing the lemon zest into the sugar with your fingertips to release the lemon oil, until the sugar is fragrant and pale yellow.

In a medium bowl, whisk the flour, baking powder, and salt to combine.

In the bowl of a stand mixer fitted with the paddle attachment, mix together the lemon sugar, sour cream, and lemon juice on low speed. Turn off the mixer and add the flour mixture, then pulse until just combined. Add the melted butter and mix until just combined into a smooth batter, 15–30 seconds.

BAKE THE CAKE

Pour the batter into the prepared cake pan, tapping the pan on the counter a few times to reduce any air bubbles. Layer the lemon slices on top, and sprinkle with the 2 tbsp sugar. Bake for 26–30 minutes, until the cake edges are lightly browned, and a toothpick inserted into the center comes out with only moist crumbs. Let the cake cool completely in its pan set on top of a wire rack.

MAKE THE VANILLA BEAN GLAZE

Combine the icing sugar, soy milk, vanilla bean paste, and salt in a small bowl and whisk until smooth. Adjust the thickness of the glaze to your liking by adding more icing sugar, 1 tbsp at a time, or soy milk, 1 tsp at a time.

ASSEMBLE THE CAKE

Remove the cooled cake from the pan. Pour the glaze over the cake and let it set for 20 minutes before slicing. Add fresh raspberries and edible flowers, if desired.

This cake will taste freshest eaten within a day of making it, but can be stored in the fridge, covered, for up to 3 days. See page 13 for storage notes.

Pumpkin Cake

- 1½ cups (210g) all-purpose flour
- 1 tsp baking powder
- 1 tsp cinnamon
- 1 tsp ground ginger
- ¾ tsp fine sea salt
- ½ cup (125ml) vegetable oil
- ¾ cup (150g) brown sugar
- ¼ cup (50g) granulated white sugar
- 1 cup (250g) pumpkin puree

Coconut Whipped Cream

- 1 cup (250ml) coconut cream, refrigerated in its can overnight
- ¼ cup (32g) icing sugar, sifted
- ½ tsp pure vanilla extract
- Pinch of salt

COZY PUMPKIN PIE CAKE

MAKES ONE 8-INCH SINGLE-LAYER CAKE

I call this pumpkin cake "cozy" because it's a very comforting, warming cake that's simple to put together. It's really moist and delicious on its own, but I also love it with a contrasting cool scoop of dairy-free vanilla ice cream (pictured), or a generous dollop of cold coconut whipped cream. Slice yourself a square for the perfect accompaniment to a cup of tea and a good book, or a healthy-ish treat in your lunchbox, or an afternoon pick-me-up. It really tastes like pumpkin pie!

MAKE THE PUMPKIN CAKE

Preheat the oven to 350°F (175°C). Prepare an 8-inch square pan by spritzing it with vegetable oil and lining with a parchment paper square cut to size, and then spritzing again with oil, to prevent sticking.

In a medium bowl, sift together the flour, baking powder, cinnamon, ginger, and salt to combine.

In the bowl of a stand mixer fitted with the paddle attachment, beat the vegetable oil, brown sugar, and white sugar on medium speed to combine, about 1 minute.

Add the flour mixture to the bowl of the stand mixer and beat on low speed until just combined, about 15 seconds. Add the pumpkin puree and mix on low speed to combine, 15–30 seconds.

BAKE THE CAKE

Pour the batter into the prepared cake pan. Give the pan a light tap on the counter to reduce any air bubbles. Bake for 23–26 minutes, until a toothpick inserted into the center comes out with only moist crumbs.

Let the cake cool slightly, 15–20 minutes, or completely in its pan set on a wire rack.

MAKE THE COCONUT WHIPPED CREAM

Place the metal bowl and whisk attachment of your stand mixer in the freezer to chill for 15–20 minutes.

Fit your stand mixer with the chilled bowl and whisk and whip the coconut cream until thickened and fluffy. Add the icing sugar, vanilla extract, and pinch of salt and beat for another minute to combine. Refrigerate until ready to serve. Coconut whipped cream can be stored in the fridge for up to 3 days.

SERVE THE CAKE

Slice the cool cake into squares. Top each slice with a generous amount of cold coconut whipped cream (or vanilla ice cream, if you prefer) and enjoy.

This cake will taste freshest eaten within a day of making it, but can be stored in the fridge, covered, for up to 3 days. See page 13 for storage notes.

Streusel

1 cup (140g) all-purpose flour

5 tbsp (75g) granulated white sugar

¾ tsp fine sea salt

6 tbsp (90g) unsalted plant-based butter, room temperature, cut into cubes

Blueberry Sour Cream Cake

¾ cup + 2 tsp (150g) granulated white sugar

1 cup (250g) plant-based sour cream

½ cup (125ml) vegetable oil

1 tsp pure vanilla extract

1 tbsp lemon zest

1½ cups (210g) all-purpose flour

1½ tsp baking powder

1 tsp fine sea salt

½ tsp baking soda

1½ cups (240g) fresh or frozen blueberries + more for serving (optional)

BLUEBERRY SOUR CREAM STREUSEL CAKE

MAKES ONE 9-INCH SINGLE-LAYER CAKE

This recipe is a blueberry 3 p.m. pick-me-up for when your afternoon is dragging by, but a leeeetle square of sweet and salty streusel-topped blueberry sour cream cake will help make your day. It's also the little snacking cake that could, perfect nestled into lunchboxes or served at brunch along with waffles, fresh fruit, and cups of hot coffee. Feel free to swap out the blueberries for raspberries, or sour cherries—whatever is in season and within your grasp! You can use frozen berries for this too.

MAKE THE STREUSEL

In a medium bowl, stir together the flour, sugar, and salt. Sprinkle in the butter pieces and toss to coat. Using your hands, rub the butter into the dry ingredients with your fingertips until it is incorporated somewhat but some floury bits remain—I like to toss it all together with my fingers, with varying sizes of streusel bits, the largest being about pea-sized. Set aside.

MAKE THE CAKE

Preheat the oven to 350°F (175°C). Prepare a 9- × 2-inch round cake pan by spritzing it with vegetable oil and lining with a parchment paper circle cut to size, and then spritzing again with oil, to prevent sticking.

In the bowl of a stand mixer fitted with the paddle attachment, mix together the sugar, sour cream, vegetable oil, vanilla extract, and lemon zest until combined.

In a medium bowl, whisk together the flour, baking powder, salt, and baking soda. Add the flour mixture to the bowl of the stand mixer, pulsing to combine, then mix on low speed for 30 seconds to form a smooth batter. Use a rubber spatula to fold in 1 cup (160g) of the blueberries, reserving the rest to add to the top of the batter.

BAKE THE CAKE

Pour the batter into the prepared cake pan, spreading and smoothing with an offset spatula if needed. Give the pan a light tap on the counter to reduce any air bubbles. Sprinkle the reserved berries on top, pushing down slightly to nestle them into the batter.

Using a large spoon, sprinkle the streusel mixture evenly over the batter.

continued

Bake for 45–50 minutes, until the streusel is getting golden brown and toasty, and a toothpick inserted into the center comes out with only moist crumbs. You can also broil the cake for 1–2 minutes at the end of the baking time (keeping a very close eye so it doesn't burn), to crisp up the streusel topping even further.

SERVE THE CAKE

Slice the cake while still in the pan, and serve warm or at room temperature, topped with fresh blueberries if you like.

This cake will taste freshest eaten within a day of making it, but can be stored in the fridge, covered, for up to 3 days. See page 13 for storage notes.

Orange Citrus Cake

2 cups (280g) all-purpose flour

1½ tsp baking powder

1 tsp baking soda

1 tsp fine sea salt

2 oranges

1 cup (200g) granulated white sugar

½ cup (125ml) vegetable oil

1 cup (250ml) soy milk

1 tsp pure vanilla extract

Orange Juice Glaze

1 cup (130g) icing sugar, sifted + more as needed

2 tbsp freshly squeezed orange juice (from the oranges listed above) + more as needed

Pinch of fine sea salt

Orange Citrus Cake with Orange Juice Glaze

MAKES ONE 8-INCH SQUARE OR 9-INCH ROUND SINGLE-LAYER CAKE

Ever had a stray, forgotten orange just rolling around in your fruit crisper drawer, on the cusp of withering? I love to salvage an almost-spoiled fruit! Sometimes I'll hold an orange in my hand and gaze at it and sniff it like an orange-loving weirdo . . . I imagine it being 100 years ago, and this prized orange is the glistening, fragrant citrus ball sitting in the bottom of my stocking on Christmas morning, the only gift I receive . . . It would be lovingly handled, carefully peeled, with each juicy segment, even the threads and white pith, treasured—and then the rinds made into candied peels so as to not waste a single little bit . . . Anyhoo! You don't need to wait until your orange is on the cusp to make this lovely cake! Choose the best-quality oranges you can, and it also works with sweet ruby red grapefruit.

MAKE THE CAKE

Preheat the oven to 350°F (175°C). Prepare an 8-inch square or 9- × 2-inch round cake pan by spritzing it with vegetable oil and lining with parchment paper cut to size, and then spritzing again with oil, to prevent sticking.

In a medium bowl, whisk together the flour, baking powder, baking soda, and salt.

Zest and then juice the oranges to make orange juice, straining out any seeds.

In the bowl of a stand mixer fitted with the paddle attachment, mix together the sugar, vegetable oil, soy milk, vanilla extract, ½ cup (125ml) orange juice (reserving the remainder for the glaze), and 2 tbsp orange zest.

Add the flour mixture to the wet mixture and pulse to combine, then mix on low speed until a smooth batter forms, 15–30 seconds.

BAKE THE CAKE

Pour the batter into the prepared cake pan, tapping the pan on the counter a few times to reduce any air bubbles. Bake for 26–30 minutes, until the cake edges are lightly browned, and a toothpick inserted into the center comes out with only moist crumbs.

Let the cake cool completely in its pan set on top of a wire rack.

MAKE THE GLAZE

In a small bowl, combine the icing sugar, reserved orange juice, and salt, whisking until smooth. Adjust the thickness of the glaze to your liking by adding small increments of icing sugar, 1 tbsp at a time, or orange juice, 1 tsp at a time.

continued

ASSEMBLE THE CAKE

Remove the cooled cake from the pan. Pour the orange juice glaze over the cake and let it set for 20 minutes before slicing. Optional decor: Cut an additional orange in half, then into thin slices. Cut out little orange triangle shapes (like tiny pizza slices) and arrange on top of the cake. Using a microplane or zester, sprinkle orange zest over the cake, if desired.

This cake will taste freshest eaten within a day of making it, but can be stored in the fridge, covered, for up to 3 days. See page 13 for storage notes.

Peanut Butter Cake

½ cup (125ml) soy milk

1 tsp apple cider vinegar

1¼ cups (175g) all-purpose flour

1½ tsp baking powder

¾ tsp baking soda

½ tsp fine sea salt

¾ cup (150g) brown sugar

6 tbsp (90ml) aquafaba (see page 8)

½ cup (125g) smooth peanut butter (see note)

½ cup (125ml) vegetable oil

1 tsp pure vanilla extract

Frosting

1 recipe Fudgy Caramel Frosting (page 139)

Flaky sea salt

PEANUT BUTTER SNACKING CAKE WITH CARAMEL FROSTING

MAKES ONE 9-INCH SINGLE-LAYER CAKE

This scrumptious snacking cake is inspired by the wonderful Yossy Arefi's peanut butter and caramel cake that our family loves so much. It was fun to "plantify" it and it's just so painfully delicious to eat—be prepared to not be able to resist slicing off little pieces of this cake all day until it's finished and you're sad that it's all gone . . . so you make another one almost immediately. It's a plush, moist peanut butter cake in a single layer, with a truly addictive salted caramel fudge-like frosting that's very simple to make on the stovetop, finished with a light sprinkle of flaky sea salt.

MAKE THE CAKE

Preheat the oven to 350°F (175°C). Prepare an 9- × 2-inch round cake pan by spritzing it with vegetable oil and lining with a parchment paper circle, and then spritzing again with oil, to prevent sticking.

In a small bowl, mix the soy milk with the apple cider vinegar and set aside for 10 minutes to thicken. It may look a bit separated at this point, but that's normal.

In a medium bowl, sift together the flour, baking powder, baking soda, and salt.

In the bowl of a stand mixer fitted with the whisk attachment, whisk together the sugar and aquafaba on medium speed until foamy. Switch to the paddle attachment and, with the mixer on low speed, add the peanut butter, mixing until smooth. Add the soy milk mixture, vegetable oil, and vanilla extract and continue mixing until combined.

With the mixer on low speed, carefully add the flour mixture and mix until smooth, 30–45 seconds. Use a spatula to fold in any stray flour lumps, but try not to overmix the batter.

BAKE THE CAKE

Pour the batter into the prepared cake pan, tapping the pan on the counter a few times to reduce any air bubbles. Bake for 26–30 minutes, until the cake edges are lightly browned, and a toothpick inserted into the center comes out with only moist crumbs.

Let the cake cool completely in its pan set on top of a wire rack.

continued

ASSEMBLE THE CAKE

Remove the cooled cake from the pan. Pour the fudgy caramel frosting onto the center of the cake and use an offset spatula to smooth it out to the edges. Sprinkle with flaky sea salt. Let the icing set for about 20 minutes before slicing.

This cake will taste freshest eaten within a day of making it, but can be stored in the fridge, covered, for up to 3 days. See page 13 for storage notes.

NOTE: For peanut butter in this recipe I tend to use the more commercial brands with added sugar; look for the brands that align with your personal values and needs. You can certainly use natural peanut butter instead, just make sure it is very well mixed and add ¼ cup extra soy milk.

Vanilla Cake

1 cup (250ml) soy milk

1 tsp apple cider vinegar

1¼ cups (175g) all-purpose flour

1 tsp baking powder

¾ tsp baking soda

½ tsp fine sea salt

¾ cup (150g) granulated white sugar

½ cup (125ml) vegetable oil

1 tbsp pure vanilla extract

1 tsp vanilla bean paste

Coffee Icing Glaze

1 tsp instant coffee granules

2 tbsp soy milk + more as needed

1 cup (130g) icing sugar + more as needed

1 tsp pure vanilla extract

Pinch of salt

VANILLA CAKE WITH COFFEE ICING GLAZE

MAKES ONE 8-INCH SINGLE-LAYER CAKE

Back when I was packing on the freshman 15 as a lazy vegetarian in my first year away at university, my dear Poh Poh would make me care packages to take back to the dorms with me. Was my Poh Poh the originator of the snacking cake? Quite possibly. Her single-layer vanilla cake was baked in a square pan and iced with a simple but addictive glaze of icing sugar, milk, and instant coffee, and the corner pieces were the most coveted—that's where the glaze met from two sides, and the fudgy icing crusted over, sugar melting in your mouth. In my second year, when I moved out of the dorms and into my own off-campus place, Poh Poh added frozen vegetable soup packed with kidney beans to the care packages (I think she was worried about my protein intake) along with the cake. Eventually she gave me a little green binder filled with her handwritten recipes to take home too—starting with the simple ones for me to tackle first—and she taught me how to bake using her ancient Mixmaster. I miss Poh Poh lots and think of her often—especially when I eat this cake!

MAKE THE CAKE

Preheat the oven to 350°F (175°C). Prepare an 8-inch square cake pan by spritzing it with vegetable oil and lining with a parchment paper square cut to size, and then spritzing again with oil, to prevent sticking.

In a small bowl, mix the soy milk with the apple cider vinegar and set aside for 10 minutes to thicken. It may look a bit separated at this point, but that's normal.

In the bowl of a stand mixer fitted with the paddle attachment, mix together the flour, baking powder, baking soda, and salt.

In a medium bowl, whisk together the soy milk mixture, sugar, vegetable oil, vanilla extract, and vanilla bean paste.

With the mixer on low speed, add the wet ingredients to the mixer and mix until combined and smooth, 30–45 seconds.

BAKE THE CAKE

Pour the batter into the prepared cake pan, tapping the pan on the counter a few times to reduce any air bubbles. Bake for 22–25 minutes, until the cake edges are lightly browned, and a toothpick inserted into the center comes out with only moist crumbs.

Let the cake cool completely in its pan set on top of a wire rack.

continued

MAKE THE COFFEE ICING GLAZE

In a small bowl, combine the instant coffee, soy milk, icing sugar, vanilla extract, and pinch of salt and whisk until smooth. Adjust the thickness of the glaze to your liking by adding small amounts of icing sugar, 1 tbsp at a time, or soy milk, 1 tsp at a time.

ASSEMBLE THE CAKE

Remove the cooled cake from the pan. Pour the glaze over the cake and let it set for 20 minutes before slicing.

This cake will taste freshest eaten within a day of making it, but can be stored in the fridge, covered, for up to 3 days. See page 13 for storage notes.

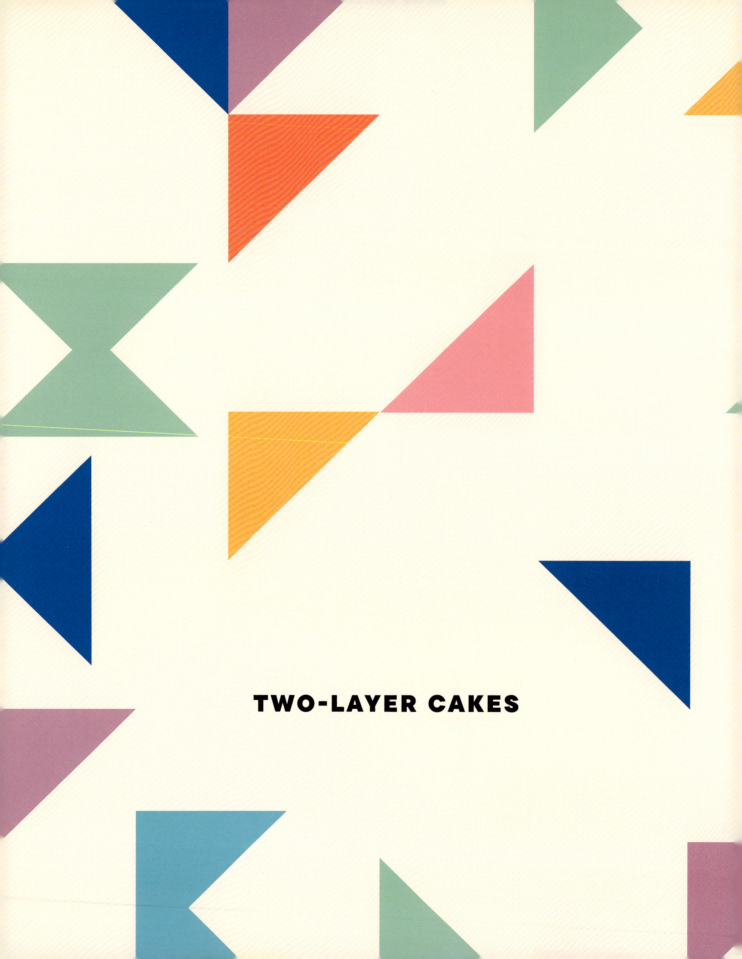
TWO-LAYER CAKES

2

"A LITTLE MORE CASUAL"

Banana Cake

1 cup (250ml) soy milk

2 tsp apple cider vinegar

3 medium super ripe bananas (375g peeled)

1 cup (200g) granulated white sugar

½ cup (125ml) vegetable oil

1 tsp pure vanilla extract

3 cups (390g) cake flour

2 tsp baking powder

1 tsp baking soda

1 tsp fine sea salt

Filling + Frosting

1 recipe Peanut Butter Frosting (page 127)

Fresh raspberries (optional)

BANANA CAKE WITH PEANUT BUTTER FROSTING

MAKES ONE 8-INCH 2-LAYER CAKE

I think we can all agree (except for those who simply hate bananas, I guess) that bananas are magical. Our yellow fruity friends are endlessly appealing, deeply flavorful, and a bonus binding ingredient! The key to a dee-licious banana cake is using super-duper-ripe bananas with tons of speckles—and even better is a completely black peel! The gooey insides will be incredibly sweet and perfect for your banana baking needs! I love sitting down to a PB+B sandwich midday, so consider this recipe the cake version.

MAKE THE CAKE

Preheat the oven to 350°F (175°C). Prepare two 8- × 2-inch round cake pans by spritzing them with vegetable oil and lining with parchment paper circles cut to size, and then spritzing again with oil, to prevent sticking.

In a small bowl, mix the soy milk with the apple cider vinegar and set aside for 10 minutes to thicken. It may look a bit separated at this point, but that's normal.

In the bowl of a stand mixer fitted with the paddle attachment, blend the bananas until they become almost liquid. Add the sugar, vegetable oil, and vanilla extract and blend to combine.

In a large bowl, sift together the cake flour, baking powder, baking soda, and salt.

With the mixer turned off, add the dry ingredients, then turn to very low speed to gently incorporate. Stream in the soy milk mixture and mix until combined and no dry streaks remain.

BAKE THE CAKE

Divide the batter evenly between the prepared cake pans. Gently tap the cake pans on the counter to counter any overzealous air bubbles. Bake for 22–25 minutes, until a toothpick inserted into the center of the cake comes out with only moist crumbs.

Let the cakes cool completely in their pans set on top of wire racks.

ASSEMBLE THE CAKE

Follow the steps on pages 19–22 to fill and frost the cake to the final frost stage, using the peanut buttercream. For this photo I used a naked style of frosting. Top with fresh raspberries.

This cake will taste freshest eaten within a day of making it, but can be stored in the fridge, covered, for up to 3 days. See page 13 for storage notes.

Vanilla Cake

3 cups (390g) cake flour

1½ cups (300g) granulated white sugar

3 tbsp baking powder

¾ tsp fine sea salt

1½ cups (375ml) soy milk

½ cup (125ml) vegetable oil

2 tsp pure vanilla extract

Filling + Frosting

Strawberry jam (page 141) or use your favorite store-bought

1 recipe Vanilla Swiss Meringue Buttercream (page 130)

8 strawberries, hulled and sliced

Fresh ripe strawberries, stems attached

STRAWBERRIES AND CREAM STRAWBERRY JAM CAKE

MAKES ONE 8-INCH 2-LAYER CAKE

I've always been envious of those lucky folks with summer birthdays. Beach parties! Swimming outdoors! Sunny sticky ice cream birthday fun! My birthday, which falls smack in the middle of cold rainy November, is Guns N' Roses "November Rain" brought to life. I can count the number of times it *hasn't* rained on my birthday, which is probably what makes me delightfully goth. Another reason summer birthdays rule: SUMMER FRUIT! Oh, the bounty. When June rolls around here in Vancouver, my husband and I get very excited, as we know it's the beginning of local strawberry season. This strawberries and cream cake has soft vanilla cake spread with strawberry jam, sliced strawberries nestled in Vanilla Swiss Meringue Buttercream (page 130), and a topping of fresh strawberries.

MAKE THE CAKE

Preheat the oven to 350°F (175°C). Prepare two 8- × 2-inch round cake pans by spritzing them with vegetable oil and lining with parchment paper circles cut to size, and then spritzing again with oil, to prevent sticking.

In the bowl of a stand mixer fitted with the paddle attachment, mix together the flour, sugar, baking powder, and salt until combined. With the mixer on low speed, add the soy milk, vegetable oil, and vanilla extract, mixing until just combined, 10–15 seconds, scraping down the sides of the bowl with a spatula if needed.

BAKE THE CAKE

Divide the cake batter evenly between the prepared pans. Give the pans a light tap on the counter to reduce any air bubbles. Bake for 23–26 minutes, or until the cake edges are lightly browned, and a toothpick inserted into the center comes out with only moist crumbs.

Let the cakes cool completely in their pans set on top of wire racks.

ASSEMBLE THE CAKE

Follow the steps on pages 19–22 to fill and frost the cake, adding a thin layer of strawberry jam to each cake layer before topping with the Vanilla Swiss Meringue Buttercream. Once the buttercream is added in a thick layer, place the sliced strawberries into the buttercream, spaced out evenly, pushing down into the buttercream to stick them in place. Add a thin layer of buttercream on top of the strawberries before placing the next cake layer on top. Add a thin layer of strawberry jam to the top layer of the cake before adding more buttercream.

Decorate the top of the cake with fresh whole strawberries.

This cake will taste freshest eaten within a day of making it, but can be stored in the fridge, covered, for up to 3 days. See page 13 for storage notes.

Vanilla Almond Cake

- 1½ cups (375ml) oat milk
- 2 tsp apple cider vinegar
- ⅓ cup (80ml) unsweetened applesauce
- ¼ cup (60ml) vegetable oil
- 2 tsp pure vanilla extract
- 3 cups (300g) extra-fine almond flour
- 1½ cups (300g) granulated white sugar
- 1 cup (190g) potato starch
- ¼ cup (30g) cornstarch
- 1½ tsp baking powder
- 1½ tsp baking soda
- 1 tsp fine sea salt

Caramel Almond Brittle

- ⅓ cup (80ml) water
- ½ cup (125ml) light corn syrup
- 1 cup (200g) granulated white sugar
- 4 tbsp (60g) unsalted plant-based butter or coconut oil
- 1 tbsp pure vanilla extract
- ¾ tsp baking soda
- ¼ tsp fine sea salt
- 1 cup (110g) sliced toasted almonds

Filling + Frosting

- 1 recipe Vanilla Bean Buttercream (page 125)

VANILLA ALMOND RASPBERRY CAKE WITH VANILLA BUTTERCREAM + CARAMEL ALMOND BRITTLE

MAKES ONE 8-INCH 2-LAYER CAKE   (GF)

This cake almost feels like it's been completely soaked in a syrup, thanks to the ultra-moist combination of almond flour, vegetable oil, and applesauce. Paired with simple vanilla frosting and studded with fresh raspberries for a juicy burst of sweet tang, it makes a delightful birthday cake for the gluten-free folks in your life. (One can never have enough raspberries, my favorite fresh pop of color for cakes.) The caramel almond brittle on top is inspired by Stella Parks's peanut brittle and adds a sugary addictive crunch. It can be added liberally like sprinkles, as well as used as angular decor in the form of shards plunked into the frosting. I like to add fresh raspberries to the top as well.

MAKE THE CAKE

Preheat the oven to 350°F (175°C). Prepare two 8- × 2-inch round cake pans by spritzing them with vegetable oil and lining with parchment paper circles cut to size, and then spritzing again with oil, to prevent sticking.

In a small bowl, mix the oat milk with the apple cider vinegar and set aside for 10 minutes to thicken. It may look a bit separated at this point, but that's normal.

In the bowl of a stand mixer fitted with the paddle attachment, combine the oat milk mixture with the applesauce, vegetable oil, and vanilla extract on low speed until combined.

In a medium bowl, sift together the almond flour, sugar, potato starch, cornstarch, baking powder, baking soda, and salt.

With the mixer turned off, add the dry ingredients. Pulse to combine and then mix on low speed until the ingredients are combined and a smooth batter forms, 15–20 seconds, scraping down the sides of the bowl as needed.

continued

BAKE THE CAKE

Divide the batter evenly between the prepared cake pans. Give the pans a light tap on the counter to reduce any air bubbles. Bake for 25–28 minutes, until a toothpick inserted into the center of the cake comes out with only moist crumbs.

Let the cakes cool completely in their pans set on top of wire racks.

MAKE THE ALMOND BRITTLE

Lightly grease a rimmed baking sheet with plant butter or coconut oil and set aside.

In a medium saucepan set over medium-low heat, whisk to combine the water, corn syrup, sugar, butter, and vanilla extract. Continue to heat, gently whisking, until the clear syrup is bubbling around the edges, about 5 minutes. Increase the heat to medium-high and cook without stirring until the syrup is a golden color and hits the caramel stage on a candy thermometer (340°F or 170°C), about 10 minutes.

Remove the caramel from the heat and stir in the baking soda and salt with a heat-resistant spatula. Stir in the sliced toasted almonds, then pour the caramel onto the baking sheet. Allow to cool to room temperature.

Using a rolling pin, crack the caramel brittle into small pieces, crushing some for a sprinkle-like consistency, and keeping other pieces large for decorative shards. Brittle will keep in an airtight container at room temperature for up to 2 weeks, or frozen for up to 6 months.

ASSEMBLE THE CAKE

Follow the steps on pages 19–21 to fill and frost the cake, using the vanilla buttercream. After frosting the first cake layer, place fresh raspberries on top of the buttercream, pushing them into the buttercream gently, then, using an offset spatula, add a thin layer of frosting on top of the raspberries to cover them. Add the second cake layer. Continue to the final frost stage. For the cake pictured here, I used the au naturel style for the second layer of frosting, but you could also try it naked.

Decorate the cake with fresh raspberries, sprinkles of shattered brittle and larger pieces of brittle sticking upright, placed in the frosting to stand up.

This cake will taste freshest eaten within a day of making it, but can be stored in the fridge, covered, for up to 3 days. See page 13 for storage notes.

Vanilla Cake

1 cup (250ml) soy milk

⅓ cup (100g) plant-based sour cream

5 tbsp (75ml) aquafaba (see page 8)

2 tsp pure vanilla extract or clear artificial vanilla extract

2¼ cups (315g) all-purpose flour

1½ cups (300g) granulated white sugar

4 tsp baking powder

½ tsp fine sea salt

¾ cup (170g) unsalted plant-based butter, room temperature

Filling + Frosting

1 recipe Pink Vanilla Buttercream (page 127)

SUPERMARKET BAKERY-STYLE CAKE WITH PINK VANILLA BUTTERCREAM

MAKES ONE 8-INCH 2-LAYER CAKE

I love peering into the bakery case under the fluorescent lights of the supermarket to see the myriad of ready-to-buy birthday and celebration cakes on display. There you'll find premade cakes mass-produced and slathered with frosting from a bucket, then piped with big colorful garish borders. This recipe reminds me of the flavor of those cakes, with its plush vanilla cake layers and simple, creamy pink vanilla buttercream. To really get that supermarket bakery flavor, swap out the pure vanilla extract for clear artificial vanilla extract!

MAKE THE CAKE

Preheat the oven to 350°F (175°C). Prepare two 8- × 2-inch round cake pans by spritzing them with vegetable oil and lining with parchment paper circles cut to size, and then spritzing again with oil, to prevent sticking.

In a large bowl, vigorously whisk the soy milk, sour cream, aquafaba, and vanilla extract together using a balloon whisk, until combined and frothy.

In the bowl of a stand mixer fitted with the paddle attachment, mix together the flour, sugar, baking powder, and salt until combined.

With the mixer on low speed, add the butter, 1-inch pieces at a time (I just use a butter knife to slice off pieces from the brick of butter right into the bowl). The mixture should clump up and look as if there are some coarse sand–like pieces in there.

With the mixer still on low speed, pour in half of the whipped milk mixture, mixing for about 15 seconds to incorporate. Pour in the remaining milk mixture and mix until a smooth batter forms, about 30 seconds.

BAKE THE CAKE

Divide the batter evenly between the prepared cake pans, evening out the batter with an offset spatula if needed. Give the pans a light tap on the counter to reduce any air bubbles. Bake for 22–25 minutes, or until the cakes are lightly golden, and a toothpick inserted in the center comes out with only moist crumbs.

Let the cakes cool completely in their pans set on top of wire racks.

continued

ASSEMBLE THE CAKE

Follow the steps on pages 19–22 to fill and frost the cake to the final frost stage, using the pink vanilla buttercream. For the second layer of frosting, I opted for a smooth style (see page 22).

Fit a piping bag with an open star tip and fill the bag with frosting. Pipe a ruffle shell border on the top edge of the cake. Dust with rainbow sprinkles. Alternately, you can make swoops in the frosting using a small offset spatula for a homemade birthday cake look.

This cake will taste freshest eaten within a day of making it, but can be stored in the fridge, covered, for up to 3 days. See page 13 for storage notes.

NOTE This cake uses the reverse-creaming method: instead of beating the butter and sugar together, you mix the dry ingredients, then you add the butter pieces, coating the fat in the flour so it resembles coarse sand. Coating the butter in flour helps to limit the formation of gluten, ensuring the end result is light and soft! Thank you Tessa Huff of *Style Sweet* for introducing me to the reverse-creaming method!

Cake

- 3 cups (420g) all-purpose flour
- 2 cups (400g) granulated white sugar
- 2 tsp baking soda
- 1 tsp kosher salt
- 1 tbsp instant espresso granules
- 1½ cups (375ml) boiling water
- ⅔ cup (80g) Dutch-process cocoa powder
- 1 cup (250ml) vegetable oil
- 1 tbsp pure vanilla extract
- ¼ cup (60ml) apple cider vinegar

Filling + Frosting

- 1 recipe Chocolate Fudge Buttercream (page 126)
- Rainbow sprinkles (optional)

Dark Chocolate Cake with Chocolate Fudge Buttercream

MAKES ONE 8-INCH 2-LAYER CAKE

This rich, dark chocolate cake has pronounced chocolate flavor in its moist tender layers, thanks to the cocoa powder blooming method—that is, heating cocoa powder in hot liquid, in this case, hot coffee! Instead of busting out the espresso maker, all you need is granulated instant espresso and boiling water. Top this cake with Chocolate Fudge Buttercream (page 126) and pair it with a tall glass of ice-cold soy milk!

MAKE THE CAKE

Preheat the oven to 350°F (175°C). Prepare two 8- × 2-inch round cake pans by spritzing them with vegetable oil and lining with parchment paper circles cut to size, and then spritzing again with oil, to prevent sticking.

In the bowl of a stand mixer fitted with the whisk attachment, whisk the flour, sugar, baking soda, and salt until combined. Switch out to the paddle attachment.

In a large bowl, whisk together the espresso powder and boiling water to combine. Whisk in the cocoa powder until combined. Whisk in the vegetable oil and vanilla extract (don't worry if it won't emulsify, it will all come together!).

Add the wet mixture to the bowl of the stand mixer and mix on low speed for about 20 seconds to combine. Add the apple cider vinegar and mix to combine, another 15 seconds, until the batter is smooth, scraping down the sides of the bowl if needed.

BAKE THE CAKE

Divide the batter evenly between the prepared cake pans. Give the pans a light tap on the counter to reduce any air bubbles. Bake for 25–28 minutes, until the cake springs back to the touch, and a toothpick inserted in the center comes back with only moist crumbs.

Let the cakes cool completely in their pans set on top of wire racks.

ASSEMBLE THE CAKE

Follow the steps on pages 19–22 to fill and frost the cake to the final frost stage, using the chocolate fudge buttercream. Finish the cake with buttercream piping or swoops of frosting and a piped border on top (see page 27), if you fancy. Adorn with sprinkles or pieces of chopped chocolate!

This cake will taste freshest eaten within a day of making it, but can be stored in the fridge, covered, for up to 3 days. See page 13 for storage notes.

THREE-LAYER CAKES

3

PARTY ANIMAL

Apple Cake

2½ cups (350g) all-purpose flour

2 tsp baking powder

1 tsp baking soda

¾ tsp fine sea salt

2 tsp ground cinnamon

1 cup (250ml) vegetable oil

½ cup (140ml) unsweetened applesauce

¾ cup (150g) light brown sugar

½ cup (100g) granulated white sugar

2 tsp pure vanilla extract

2 cups (300g) grated apple

Oatmeal Cookie Crumbles

5 tbsp (75g) granulated white sugar

¾ cup (75g) rolled oats

⅓ cup (46g) all-purpose flour

½ tsp fine sea salt

4 tbsp (60g) unsalted plant-based butter, room temperature, cut into cubes

Frosting

1 recipe Salted Caramel Buttercream (page 126) (reserve some of the salted caramel to decorate the cake)

APPLE CARAMEL CAKE WITH OATMEAL COOKIE CRUMBLES

MAKES ONE 7-INCH 3-LAYER CAKE

Red and orange autumn leaves, shiny apples plucked from trees—and a slice of apple caramel cake for meeee! Haha. Many years ago when I was an office temp receptionist, one of my favorite "let's make my day better" power moves was packing a Granny Smith apple in my lunch along with a generous handful of caramel squares. Take a crunchy bite of apple, pop a chewy soft caramel in your mouth, and you've got instant caramel apple! In this recipe, freshly grated apple cake and caramel buttercream team up with oatmeal cookie crumbles to create a perfect fall vibes cake. Bonus: leftover oatmeal cookie crumbles are a sheer delight layered in yogurt parfaits or liberally sprinkled on top of ice cream.

MAKE THE CAKE

Preheat the oven to 350°F (175°C). Prepare three 7- × 2-inch round cake pans by spritzing them with vegetable oil and lining with parchment paper circles cut to size. Spray again with oil to prevent sticking.

In a medium bowl, whisk together the flour, baking powder, baking soda, salt, and cinnamon.

In the bowl of a stand mixer fitted with the paddle attachment, combine the vegetable oil, applesauce, brown sugar, white sugar, and vanilla extract on medium speed until smooth, about 1 minute.

With the mixer on low speed, add the dry ingredients, mixing until combined, 15–30 seconds. Fold in the grated apple.

BAKE THE CAKE

Divide the cake batter evenly between the prepared pans. Give the pans a light tap on the counter to reduce any air bubbles. Bake for 22–25 minutes, until the cake edges are lightly browned, the cake springs back to the touch, and a toothpick inserted into the center comes out with only moist crumbs.

Let the cakes cool completely in their pans set on top of wire racks.

continued

MAKE THE OATMEAL COOKIE CRUMBLES

Preheat the oven to 350°F (175°). Line a baking sheet with parchment paper.

In a medium bowl, whisk together the sugar, rolled oats, flour, and salt. Sprinkle in the butter, toss to coat, and then mix until well incorporated.

Using a spatula, spread the mixture onto the prepared baking sheet in an even layer. Bake for 18–20 minutes, until golden brown and crisp. Let cool completely in its pan set on top of a wire rack.

Once cooled, break up into cookie crumbles with your hands or lightly bash it with a rolling pin.

ASSEMBLE THE CAKE

Follow the steps on pages 19–22 to fill and frost the cake using the salted caramel buttercream. While building the cake layers, follow the dugout pool method to carve out a small pool in the center of the buttercream and add some extra salted caramel to the layers. Continue on until the final frost stage. For the photo opposite, I used an au naturel style for the second layer of frosting.

DECORATE THE CAKE

Decorate the cake with a piped salted caramel buttercream border on top, or an artful array of piped dollops or drop stars (see page 27). You can also add drips of salted caramel to the outside of the cake. To preserve maximum crispness, add the oatmeal cookie crumbles in various-sized pieces to the top of the cake just before serving!

This cake will taste freshest enjoyed within a day of making it, but can be stored in the fridge, covered, for up to 3 days. See page 13 for more storage notes.

Banana Cake

1 cup (250ml) soy milk

2 tsp apple cider vinegar

3 medium super ripe bananas (you're aiming for 375g peeled)

1 cup (200g) granulated white sugar

¾ cup (185ml) vegetable oil

1 tsp pure vanilla extract

3 cups (390g) cake flour

2 tsp baking powder

1 tsp baking soda

1 tsp fine sea salt

Toffee Crunch

1 cup (224g) unsalted plant-based butter

1¼ cups (250g) granulated white sugar

1 tbsp pure maple syrup

½ cup (125ml) soy milk

1 tsp fine sea salt

Filling + Frosting

1 recipe Chocolate Ganache Frosting (page 139)

1 recipe Salted Caramel Buttercream (page 126) (reserve ½ cup/125ml of the salted caramel for soaking and decorating the cake)

BANANA CARAMEL CAKE WITH SALTED CARAMEL BUTTERCREAM + CARAMEL DRIPS

MAKES ONE 7-INCH 3-LAYER CAKE

Being the daughter of a fruit and vegetable wholesaler, I had an array of delightfully campy banana-themed promotional goods as a child. Banana-horned stuffed unicorns, XXL Chiquita Banana T-shirts, banana storage-temperature thermometer signs, and our most prized and well-used item: a Chiquita Banana picnic blanket! But I really am fond of bananas. This moist banana cake has creamy chocolate ganache and salted caramel buttercream united in one bonkers delicious cake. Plus, it's topped with an addictive toffee crunch and salted caramel drips. If the components feel a little too bananas to make all in one day, you can break up the recipe by baking the cake, preparing the salted caramel, and whipping up the toffee crunch (note: you'll need a candy thermometer!) one or two days ahead of assembling the cake.

MAKE THE CAKE

Preheat the oven to 350°F (175°C). Prepare three 7- × 2-inch round cake pans by spritzing them with vegetable oil and lining with parchment paper circles cut to size, and then spritzing again with oil, to prevent sticking.

In a small bowl, mix the soy milk with the apple cider vinegar and set aside for 10 minutes to thicken. It may look a bit separated at this point, but that's normal.

In the bowl of a stand mixer fitted with the paddle attachment, blend the bananas until they become almost liquid. Add the sugar, vegetable oil, and vanilla extract and blend to combine.

In a large bowl, sift together the flour, baking powder, baking soda, and salt.

With the mixer turned off, add the dry ingredients, then turn to very low speed to gently incorporate. Stream in the soy milk mixture. Mix, scraping down the sides of the bowl if necessary, until combined and no dry streaks remain, about 30 seconds.

continued

BAKE THE CAKE

Divide the batter evenly between the prepared cake pans. Gently tap the cake pans on the counter to counter any overzealous air bubbles. Bake for 22–25 minutes, until a toothpick inserted into the center of the cake comes out with only moist crumbs.

Let the cakes cool completely in their pans set on top of wire racks.

MAKE THE TOFFEE CRUNCH

Line a baking sheet with parchment paper. Get your apron on and oven mitts ready—she's a hot one!

In a heavy-bottomed pot set over medium-high heat, combine the butter, sugar, maple syrup, soy milk, and salt, stirring constantly and melting everything together, until the mixture begins to boil, being careful nothing boils over!

Continue stirring until the mixture reaches the "soft crack" stage as measured with a candy thermometer, approximately 275°F–290°F (135°C–143°C). Immediately pour the candy mixture onto the prepared baking sheet, spreading it out with an offset spatula to the edges of the parchment paper. Let cool completely before breaking up into differently sized toffee pieces. Store leftover toffee in an airtight container for up to 1 week.

ASSEMBLE THE CAKE

Follow the steps on pages 19–22 to fill the cake with the chocolate ganache frosting and frost with the salted caramel buttercream to the final frost stage. While building the cake, soak the cake layers with salted caramel, then follow the dugout pool method to add some extra chocolate ganache to the layers. For the photo opposite, I used a smooth style for my second layer of frosting.

DECORATE THE CAKE

Using a spoon, add some salted caramel drips to the cake, starting with a very small amount of caramel to test the drips. Finish the cake with some salted caramel buttercream piping details (try artful dollops or drop stars), and some deliberately placed toffee shards. Finish with a sprinkling of toffee pieces.

This cake will taste freshest enjoyed within a day of making it, but can be stored in the fridge, covered, for up to 3 days. See page 13 for more storage notes.

Vanilla Bean Cake

1¼ cups (310ml) soy milk

2 tsp apple cider vinegar

½ cup (125ml) aquafaba (see page 8)

½ cup (112g) unsalted plant-based butter, room temperature

½ cup (125ml) vegetable oil

1½ cups (300g) granulated white sugar

1 tbsp pure vanilla extract

Seeds from 1 whole vanilla bean pod or 2 tbsp vanilla bean paste

3 cups (390g) cake flour

1 tbsp baking powder

1 tsp baking soda

1 tsp fine sea salt

Passion Fruit Syrup

½ cup (100g) passion fruit pulp (6–7 passion fruit) (see note)

1 cup (250ml) water

1 cup (200g) granulated white sugar

Caramel Crunch

⅓ cup (80ml) water

½ cup (125ml) light corn syrup

1 cup (200g) granulated white sugar

4 tbsp (60g) unsalted plant-based butter

1 tbsp pure vanilla extract

¾ tsp baking soda

¼ tsp fine sea salt

Filling + Frosting

1 recipe Passion Fruit Vanilla Swiss Meringue Buttercream (page 132)

Gel color of your choice (I used teal here, but a pink/orange/yellow ombré effect would also be beautiful)

PASSION FRUIT VANILLA BEAN OMBRÉ CAKE WITH CARAMEL CRUNCH

MAKES ONE 7-INCH 3-LAYER CAKE

For my sister Leanne's milestone birthday, I made this passion fruit syrup–soaked vanilla bean cake with passion fruit Swiss meringue buttercream and textural caramel crunch, frosted in an ombré teal pattern. For the fresh floral blooms, I wrapped each stem in plastic wrap and arranged them on top by inserting into the buttercream. This is the perfect cake for a special birthday celebration, or you could make a trio of these for wedding cakes in different colors.

NOTE If you can't find fresh passion fruit (tip: they look dry and wrinkly when they're ripe!), frozen passion fruit pulp can be found at many specialty or diverse grocery stores. Or you can substitute Vanilla Bean Buttercream (page 125) with added freeze-dried passion fruit powder, which can be found at gourmet food shops, or online.

MAKE THE CAKE

Preheat the oven to 350°F (175°C). Prepare three 7- × 2-inch round cake pans by spritzing them with vegetable oil and lining with parchment paper circles cut to size, and then spritzing again with oil, to prevent sticking.

In a small bowl, mix the soy milk with the apple cider vinegar and set aside for 10 minutes to thicken. It may look a bit separated at this point, but that's normal.

In a small bowl, whisk the aquafaba until foamy and light, about 1 minute, and set aside.

In the bowl of a stand mixer fitted with the paddle attachment, cream together the butter, vegetable oil, and sugar until creamy and blended well. Add the foamy aquafaba, vanilla extract, and vanilla bean paste, mixing until combined.

continued

PARTY ANIMAL THREE-LAYER CAKES   89

In a large bowl, whisk together the cake flour, baking powder, baking soda, and salt.

With the mixer on low speed, alternate between adding the flour mixture and soy milk mixture, beginning and ending with the flour mixture, until just combined. Do not overmix. Use a spatula to fold in any stray flour lumps, but try not to overmix the batter.

BAKE THE CAKE

Divide the cake batter evenly between the prepared pans. Give the pans a light tap on the counter to reduce any air bubbles. Bake for 22–25 minutes, until the cake edges are lightly browned, and a toothpick inserted into the center comes out with only moist crumbs.

Let the cakes cool completely in their pans set on top of wire racks.

MAKE THE PASSION FRUIT SYRUP

In a small saucepan set over medium-high heat, bring the passion fruit pulp, water, and sugar to a boil. Reduce the heat to low and simmer until the syrup has reduced by half. Strain the syrup into a clean, empty jar. Let cool completely and refrigerate if not using right away.

MAKE THE CARAMEL CRUNCH

Lightly grease a rimmed baking sheet with plant-based butter or coconut oil and set aside.

In a medium saucepan set over medium-low heat, whisk the water, corn syrup, sugar, butter, and vanilla extract until combined. Continue to gently whisk until the clear syrup is bubbling around the edges, about 5 minutes. Increase the heat to medium-high and cook without stirring until the syrup is a golden color and hits the caramel stage on a candy thermometer (340°F/170°C), about 10 minutes.

Remove the caramel from the heat and stir in the baking soda and salt with a heat-resistant spatula, then pour the caramel onto the prepared baking sheet. Cool completely to room temperature.

When cool, using a rolling pin, crack the caramel into small pieces, crushing it up for a sprinkle-like consistency. Caramel crunch will keep for up to 2 weeks in an airtight container at room temperature or frozen for up to 6 months.

ASSEMBLE THE CAKE

Using a cake turntable if possible, follow the steps on pages 19–22 to fill and frost the cake with the passion fruit vanilla Swiss meringue buttercream, to the final frost stage. Add a generous amount of passion fruit syrup first to each layer as you build the cake. And add a generous sprinkle of caramel crunch on top of each buttercream layer too, pressing it into the buttercream.

To create an ombré colored effect for the final buttercream coat, divide the remaining buttercream between three bowls. Tint the first bowl with ½ tsp teal gel color, the second bowl with ⅛ tsp teal gel color, and leave the third as is.

Fit three piping bags each with an open circle tip and fill each bag with one color of buttercream. Starting with the darkest shade of teal, pipe two or three rows of frosting in a continuous line around the whole cake, starting from the bottom of the cake. Then pipe the less-teal buttercream in two or three more rows above the first. Finally, pipe the remaining white buttercream in more rows until you reach the top of the cake.

With the cake placed on your cake turntable, slowly turn the cake, using a bench scraper to scrape the sides of the cake in one continuous motion to create three stripes of buttercream. Keep scraping until you are happy with the look of the ombré effect. If you like, use an offset spatula to press into the buttercream stripes, starting from the bottom of the cake and working your way up, to create the rustic look pictured here.

Finish with fresh flowers (wrap the stems in plastic wrap to prevent them touching the cake).

This cake will taste freshest eaten within a day of making it, but can be stored in the fridge, covered, for up to 3 days. See page 13 for storage notes.

Vanilla Funfetti Cake

1¼ cups (310ml) soy milk

2 tsp apple cider vinegar

½ cup (125ml) aquafaba (see page 8)

½ cup (112g) unsalted plant-based butter, room temperature

½ cup (125ml) vegetable oil

1½ cups (300g) granulated white sugar

1 tbsp pure vanilla extract

1 tsp vanilla bean paste

3 cups (390g) cake flour

1 tbsp baking powder

1 tsp baking soda

1 tsp fine sea salt

1½ cups (150g) rainbow sprinkles

Birthday Cake Crumbles

½ cup (100g) granulated white sugar

1 tbsp golden brown sugar

¾ cup (96g) cake flour

½ tsp baking powder

½ tsp fine sea salt

2 tbsp rainbow sprinkles

¼ cup (60ml) vegetable oil

1 tsp pure vanilla extract

Filling + Frosting

1 recipe Vanilla Buttercream (page 125)

Rainbow sprinkles, for sprinkling

FUNFETTI CAKE WITH VANILLA BUTTERCREAM AND BIRTHDAY CAKE CRUMBLES

MAKES ONE 7-INCH 3-LAYER CAKE

The partiest party time cake! "Funfetti" is a bit of a hilarious mash-up word, taking the unique phenomenon of confetti as its base—I'll always love the idea of tiny rainbow paper bits sprinkling down from the sky in celebratory jubilation! This cake has soft, rainbow funfetti cake layers frosted with creamy nostalgic vanilla buttercream, and topped further with funfetti birthday cake crumbles inspired by Milk Bar. Serve it with scoops of vanilla ice cream for your next birthday party, and the kids (or your inner child, hehe) will be over the moon. Make sure you use the vibrant sprinkles (not all-natural colored) for baking into this cake; all-natural sprinkles may melt into the cake and not have the funfetti vibes we're going for—but they're perfect to sprinkle on the finished cake!

MAKE THE CAKE

Preheat the oven to 350°F (175°C). Prepare three 7- × 2-inch round cake pans by spritzing them with vegetable oil and lining with parchment paper circles cut to size, and then spritzing again with oil, to prevent sticking.

In a small bowl, mix the soy milk with the apple cider vinegar for about 15 seconds. Set aside for 5 minutes to thicken. It may look a bit separated at this point, but that's normal.

In a small bowl, whisk the aquafaba until foamy and light, about 1 minute, and set aside.

In the bowl of a stand mixer fitted with the paddle attachment, cream together the butter, vegetable oil, and sugar until creamy and blended well. Add the foamy aquafaba, vanilla extract, and vanilla bean paste, mixing until combined.

continued

In a large bowl, whisk together the cake flour, baking powder, baking soda, and salt.

With the mixer on low speed, alternate between adding the flour mixture and the soy milk mixture, beginning and ending with the flour mixture, until just combined. Do not overmix. Use a spatula to fold in any stray lumps of flour, but try not to overmix the batter. At the very end, add the sprinkles and very gently fold them into the batter, about three to four turns.

BAKE THE CAKE

Divide the cake batter evenly between the prepared pans. Give the pans a light tap on the counter to reduce any air bubbles. Bake for 22–25 minutes, until the cake edges are lightly browned, and a toothpick inserted into the center comes out with only moist crumbs.

Let the cakes cool completely in their pans set on top of wire racks.

MAKE THE BIRTHDAY CAKE CRUMBLES

Preheat the oven to 300°F (150°C). Line a baking sheet with parchment paper.

In a medium bowl, combine the white sugar, brown sugar, flour, baking powder, salt, and sprinkles, mixing until combined. Add the vegetable oil and vanilla extract, mixing until small clumps of crumble form.

Spread out evenly on the prepared baking sheet. Bake for 15–20 minutes, until lightly browned and baked through.

Let cool completely before using. Break up any larger pieces if necessary.

ASSEMBLE THE CAKE

Follow the steps on pages 19–22 to fill and frost the cake with the vanilla buttercream, to the final frost stage.

Fit a piping bag with a large open star tip and fill the bag with the remaining buttercream. Pipe a ruffle or shell border around the top and bottom of the cake (see page 27). Fill the center of the border at the top of the cake with birthday cake crumbles and finish the whole cake with a generous dusting of rainbow sprinkles.

This cake will taste freshest eaten within a day of making it, but can be stored in the fridge, covered, for up to 3 days. See page 13 for storage notes.

Vanilla Cake

1¼ cups (310ml) soy milk

2 tsp apple cider vinegar

½ cup (125ml) aquafaba (see page 8)

½ cup (112g) unsalted plant-based butter, room temperature

½ cup (125ml) vegetable oil

1½ cups (300g) granulated white sugar

1 tbsp pure vanilla extract

1 tsp vanilla bean paste

3 cups (390g) cake flour

1 tbsp baking powder

1 tsp baking soda

1 tsp fine sea salt

Filling + Frosting

1 recipe Vanilla Swiss Meringue Buttercream (page 130) (and add an extra ½ tsp vanilla bean paste)

Fresh fruit (I use muscat grapes, raspberries, blackberries, and strawberries), for decor

Edible rose petals, for decor

Herbs, such as fresh mint or sage, for decor

VANILLA FRUIT + FLOWERS CAKE WITH VANILLA BEAN SWISS MERINGUE BUTTERCREAM

MAKES ONE 7-INCH 3-LAYER CAKE

As a kid, I used to think ordering vanilla ice cream or vanilla cake was . . . so vanilla. How young and silly I was. I remember making fun of an older uncle for ordering VANILLA ice cream at a place with over 100 flavors when he could have got BUBBLEGUM, or COTTON CANDY, or ROCKY ROAD!—a.k.a. all the tooth-achingly sweet flavors and bright colors that many kids love but adults may find a little too saccharine in their older and wiser age. I don't quite know how vanilla got the bad reputation, because as we all know, vanilla is DELICIOUS! Now I'm the old nerd who loves vanilla—and this cake is perfect for folks like me! Soft, fragrant vanilla cake layers and a not-too-sweet vanilla Swiss meringue buttercream. And I made this one extra pretty, covered in fruit and flowers, making it beautiful for a birthday celebration at any age.

MAKE THE CAKE

Preheat the oven to 350°F (175°C). Prepare three 7- × 2-inch round cake pans by spritzing them with vegetable oil and lining with parchment paper circles cut to size, and then spritzing again with oil, to prevent sticking.

In a small bowl, mix the soy milk with the apple cider vinegar and set aside for 10 minutes to thicken. It may look a bit separated at this point, but that's normal.

In a small bowl, whisk the aquafaba until foamy and light, about 1 minute, and set aside.

In the bowl of a stand mixer fitted with the paddle attachment, cream together the butter, vegetable oil, and sugar until creamy and blended well. Add the foamy aquafaba, vanilla extract, and vanilla bean paste, mixing until combined.

In a large bowl, whisk together the cake flour, baking powder, baking soda, and salt.

With the mixer on low speed, alternate between adding the flour mixture and the soy milk mixture, beginning and ending with the flour mixture, until just combined. Do not overmix. Use a spatula to fold in any stray flour lumps, but try not to overmix the batter.

continued

BAKE THE CAKE

Divide the cake batter evenly between the prepared pans. Give the pans a light tap on the counter to reduce any air bubbles. Bake for 22–25 minutes, until the cake edges are lightly browned, and a toothpick inserted into the center comes out with only moist crumbs.

Let the cakes cool completely in their pans set on top of wire racks.

ASSEMBLE THE CAKES

Follow the steps on pages 19–22 to fill and frost the cake using the vanilla Swiss meringue buttercream, to the final frost stage. Finish the cake with an au naturel second layer of frosting.

Fit a piping bag with a multi-pronged open star tip (or tip of your choice) and fill the bag with remaining buttercream. Pipe drop stars on top of the cake, alternating with the fresh fruit and edible rose petals.

This cake will taste freshest eaten within a day of making it, but can be stored in the fridge, covered, for up to 3 days. See page 13 for storage notes.

Strawberry Cake

3 cups (390g) cake flour

3 cups (100g) freeze-dried strawberries

1 tbsp baking powder

1 tsp baking soda

1 tsp fine sea salt

3 cups (about 300g) ripe, fresh hulled strawberries

1 cup (250ml) vegetable oil

2 cups (400g) granulated white sugar

10 tbsp (150ml) aquafaba (see page 8)

2 tsp pink natural food coloring powder or ¼ tsp pink gel color (optional)

Filling + Frosting

1 recipe Strawberry Swiss Meringue Buttercream (page 132)

Fresh sliced strawberries (optional)

STRAWBERRY DREAM CAKE WITH STRAWBERRY SWISS MERINGUE BUTTERCREAM

MAKES ONE 7-INCH 3-LAYER CAKE

This strawberry cake feels like log-rolling down a gentle grassy hill with flowers in your hair and the golden sun shining softly on your face—basically summer on a platter! A mix of pureed strawberries and freeze-dried strawberries are the key to this powerhouse of strawberry flavor, and the pink strawberry Swiss meringue buttercream tastes just like strawberry ice cream! If you want to make your strawberry cake more pink, you can add 2 tsp of pink natural food coloring powder to the food processor when you're blitzing the cake flour and freeze-dried strawberries, or add pink gel color to the cake batter!

MAKE THE CAKE

Preheat the oven to 350°F (175°C). Prepare three 7- × 2-inch round cake pans by spritzing them with vegetable oil and lining with parchment paper circles cut to size, and then spritzing again with oil, to prevent sticking.

In a food processor, blend together the cake flour and freeze-dried strawberries into a fine pink flour. Pour into a large bowl and whisk in the baking powder, baking soda, and salt. Set aside.

Using an immersion blender or regular blender, puree the fresh strawberries until liquefied.

In the bowl of a stand mixer fitted with the paddle attachment, beat the vegetable oil, sugar, aquafaba, and pink natural food coloring powder or gel color on medium-high speed until emulsified and volume has been added.

With the mixer off, add a third of the pink flour and turn the mixer to low speed to incorporate for a few seconds. Stream in a third of the pureed strawberry liquid. Repeat with the remaining pink flour and pureed strawberries, mixing on low speed for a total of 30 seconds. Turn off the mixer and finish mixing by hand using a spatula to gently and fully incorporate.

BAKE THE CAKE

Divide the batter evenly between the prepared cake pans. Gently tap the pans a few times on the counter to reduce any air bubbles, and then place in the oven. Bake for 23–27 minutes, or until the cakes are lightly golden around the edges, and a toothpick inserted in the center of the cake comes out with only moist crumbs.

Let the cakes cool completely in their pans set on top of wire racks.

ASSEMBLE THE CAKE

Follow the steps on pages 19–22 to fill and frost the cake with the strawberry Swiss meringue buttercream, to the final frost stage. Add fresh sliced strawberries to each buttercream layer before stacking the next cake on top. Finish the cake with a smooth second layer of buttercream, and top with some buttercream piping details and more fresh strawberry slices.

This cake will taste freshest eaten within a day of making it, but can be stored in the fridge, covered, for up to 3 days. See page 13 for storage notes.

Dark Chocolate Cake

3 cups (420g) all-purpose flour

2 cups (400g) granulated white sugar

2 tsp baking soda

1 tsp kosher salt

1½ cups (375ml) boiling water

1 tbsp instant espresso granules

⅔ cup (80g) Dutch-process cocoa powder

1 cup (250ml) vegetable oil

1 tbsp pure vanilla extract

¼ cup (60ml) apple cider vinegar

Filling + Frosting

1 recipe Vanilla Buttercream (page 125)

24 Oreo cookies, chopped into various sizes

COOKIES AND CREAM CAKE

MAKES ONE 7-INCH 3-LAYER CAKE

Cookies and cream, the OG favorite flavor of children everywhere (and, secretly, all of us). I think I can recall the big entry of cookies and cream into the ice cream world in the 1980s, but now it is *ubiquitous*, because the "cookie" of the cookies and cream combo is none other than the painfully addictive Oreo cookie. The not-too-sweet thin dark chocolate cookie layers sandwich a white crème filling between them, making the perfect packaged cookie. And vegans worldwide can rejoice in the fact that the Oreo is also accidentally vegan! Yeah! This cookies and cream cake does not hold back on the use of Oreos—they're chopped up into the buttercream layers and sprinkled and placed in between piped buttercream dollops, combined with dark chocolate cake layers and creamy vanilla buttercream.

MAKE THE CAKE

Preheat the oven to 350°F (175°C). Prepare three 7- × 2-inch round cake pans by spritzing them with vegetable oil and lining with parchment paper circles cut to size, and then spritzing again with oil, to prevent sticking.

In the bowl of a stand mixer fitted with the whisk attachment, whisk the flour, sugar, baking soda, and salt until combined. Switch to the paddle attachment.

In a large bowl, combine the boiling water and espresso powder and whisk to combine. Whisk in the cocoa powder until combined. Whisk in the vegetable oil and vanilla extract (don't worry if it won't emulsify, it will all come together!).

Add the wet mixture to the bowl of the stand mixer and mix on low speed for about 20 seconds to combine. Add the apple cider vinegar and mix for another 15 seconds, until the batter is smooth, scraping down the sides of the bowl if needed.

BAKE THE CAKE

Divide the batter evenly between the prepared cake pans. Give the pans a light tap on the counter to reduce any air bubbles. Bake for 22–25 minutes, until the cake springs back to the touch, and a toothpick inserted in the center comes back with only moist crumbs.

continued

ASSEMBLE THE CAKE

Follow the steps on pages 19–22 to fill and frost the cake using the vanilla buttercream, to the final frost stage. To fill the cake layers, pipe a thick layer of the vanilla buttercream on each layer first, then press chopped-up Oreo cookie pieces into the buttercream in even intervals, pushing them down into the buttercream. Add another thin layer of buttercream over the Oreo pieces, before placing the next layer of cake carefully on top. For the photo opposite, I used a smooth style for my second layer of frosting.

Decorate the top of the cake with a piped spiral border or an artful array of piped dollops, drop stars, and chopped Oreo pieces in varying sizes, or a border of piped buttercream dollops alternating with whole sandwich cookies, as I did for the photo opposite.

This cake will taste freshest eaten within a day of making it, but can be stored in the fridge, covered, for up to 3 days. See page 13 for storage notes.

Vanilla Coffee Cake

- 1¼ cups (310ml) soy milk
- 1 tbsp instant coffee granules
- ½ cup (125ml) aquafaba (see page 8)
- ½ cup (112g) unsalted plant-based butter, room temperature
- ½ cup (125ml) vegetable oil
- 1½ cups (300g) granulated white sugar
- 1 tbsp pure vanilla extract
- 1 tsp vanilla bean paste (optional)
- 1 tsp coffee-flavored extract
- 3 cups (390g) cake flour
- 1 tbsp baking powder
- 1 tsp fine sea salt

Coffee Milk Soak

- 1 cup (250ml) soy milk
- 1 tbsp instant coffee granules

Filling + Frosting

- Raspberry jam (page 141) or use your favorite store-bought
- 1 recipe Coffee Swiss Meringue Buttercream (page 131)
- Fresh raspberries

COFFEE MILK CAKE WITH COFFEE SWISS MERINGUE BUTTERCREAM + RASPBERRIES

MAKES ONE 7-INCH 3-LAYER CAKE

As a kid, I always loved the sweet, bitter, and complex flavor of coffee ice cream—I was a weird little child, I know. I was introduced to the flavor by my mom, as every Christmas, she would make her signature "Mud Pie"—which was not made of *actual* mud but was in fact a layered ice cream pie featuring a chocolate Oreo cookie crust and creamy coffee ice cream filling, topped with homemade chocolate fudge and billowy whipped cream. For this cake, I wanted to combine coffee milk–soaked cake layers with coffee buttercream and raspberries for a dream combination where sweet, tangy berries meet creamy coffee frosting.

MAKE THE CAKE

Preheat the oven to 350°F (175°C). Prepare three 7- × 2-inch round cake pans by spritzing them with vegetable oil and lining with parchment paper circles cut to size, and then spritzing again with oil, to prevent sticking.

In a small bowl or liquid measuring cup, combine the soy milk and instant coffee granules, mixing until dissolved. Set aside.

In a small bowl, whisk the aquafaba until foamy and light, about 1 minute, and set aside.

In the bowl of a stand mixer fitted with the paddle attachment, cream together the butter, vegetable oil, and sugar until creamy and blended well. Add the foamy aquafaba, vanilla extract, vanilla bean paste, and coffee extract, mixing until combined.

In a large bowl, whisk together the flour, baking powder, and salt.

With the mixer on low speed, alternate between adding the flour mixture and the coffee milk, beginning and ending with the flour mixture, until just combined. Do not overmix. Use a spatula to fold in any stray flour lumps, but try not to overmix the batter.

continued

BAKE THE CAKE

Divide the cake batter evenly between the prepared pans. Give the pans a light tap on the counter to reduce any air bubbles. Bake for 22–25 minutes, until the cake edges are lightly browned, and a toothpick inserted into the center comes out with only moist crumbs.

Let the cakes cool completely in their pans set on top of wire racks.

MAKE THE COFFEE MILK SOAK

In a small bowl or liquid measuring cup, combine the soy milk and coffee granules, mixing until dissolved.

ASSEMBLE THE CAKE

Follow the steps on pages 19–22 to fill and frost the cake using the raspberry jam and coffee Swiss meringue buttercream, to the final frost stage. Before adding the jam or frosting to each layer, soak the cake layer with the coffee milk. While building the cake layers, follow the dugout pool method to carve out a small pool in the center of the buttercream and add some raspberry jam to the layers. Alternately, you can pipe a buttercream dam around the edge of your cake (see page 19).

Decorate the cake with a piped artful array of ruffly drop stars or dollops and top with fresh raspberries.

This cake will taste freshest eaten within a day of making it, but can be stored in the fridge, covered, for up to 3 days. See page 13 for storage notes.

106   PLANTCAKES

Chocolate Cake

1 cup (250ml) soy milk

1 tsp apple cider vinegar

2 cups (400g) granulated white sugar

1¾ cups (245g) all-purpose flour

1 cup (120g) Dutch-process cocoa powder

2 tsp baking soda

1 tsp baking powder

1 tsp fine sea salt

½ cup (125ml) vegetable oil

2 tsp pure vanilla extract

1 cup (250ml) strong, hot coffee

Peanut Butter Cup Crunch

⅓ cup (80ml) water

½ cup (125ml) light corn syrup

1 cup (200g) granulated white sugar

4 tbsp (60g) unsalted plant-based butter or coconut oil

1 tbsp + 2 tsp pure vanilla extract

¾ tsp baking soda

½ tsp fine sea salt

1 cup (110g) chopped dry roasted peanuts + extra for sprinkling

¾ cup (190g) smooth peanut butter (see note on page 62)

2½ cups (450g) finely chopped bittersweet or dark plant-based chocolate

Filling + Frosting

Strawberry jam (page 141) or use your favorite store-bought

1 recipe Peanut Butter Swiss Meringue Buttercream (page 131)

Fresh strawberries

PB+J CHOCOLATE CAKE WITH PEANUT BUTTER CUP CRUNCH

MAKES ONE 7-INCH 3-LAYER CAKE

Salty-sweet peanut butter slathered with a big bright dollop of tangy jam, sandwiched between soft fresh bread—it's comfort eating at its easiest and finest, and it reminds me of my favorite childhood (and adulthood, hehe) sandwich. I made this PB+J chocolate cake for myself on my birthday a few years ago and have never looked back! Moist chocolate cake layers, Peanut Butter Swiss Meringue Buttercream (page 131), and strawberry jam filling (either homemade or store-bought) are sprinkled liberally with peanut butter cup crunch and freeze-dried strawberries to maximize the PB+J flavor blast! The peanut butter cup crunch recipe is adapted from the wonderful Stella Parks's cookbook *BraveTart*. It will make a lot of extra crunch, but you will want to eat this all day and night. For the peanut butter cup crunch, be sure to use a smooth processed commercial brand.

MAKE THE CAKE

Preheat the oven to 350°F (175°C). Prepare three 7- × 2-inch round cake pans by spritzing them with vegetable oil and lining with parchment paper circles cut to size, and then spritzing again with oil, to prevent sticking.

In a small bowl, mix the soy milk with the apple cider vinegar for about 15 seconds. Set aside for 5 minutes to thicken. It may look a bit separated at this point, but that's normal.

In the bowl of a stand mixer fitted with the paddle attachment, mix the sugar, flour, cocoa powder, baking soda, baking powder, and salt on low speed until combined.

In a medium bowl, whisk together the soy milk mixture, vegetable oil, and vanilla extract.

continued

With the mixer on low speed, add the wet ingredients to the bowl. Pour in the hot coffee and mix until combined and a smooth batter forms, 15–30 seconds, scraping down the sides of the bowl as needed.

BAKE THE CAKE

Divide the batter evenly between the prepared cake pans. Tap each pan gently on the counter to reduce any air bubbles. Bake for 22–25 minutes, or until the cake is lightly domed and has pulled away from the sides slightly, and a toothpick inserted into the center comes out with only moist crumbs.

Let the cakes cool completely in their pans set on top of wire racks.

MAKE THE PEANUT BUTTER CUP CRUNCH

Lightly grease a rimmed baking sheet with plant butter or coconut oil and set aside.

In a medium saucepan set over medium-low heat, whisk the water, corn syrup, sugar, butter, and 1 tbsp of the vanilla extract until combined. Continue to gently whisk until the clear syrup is bubbling around the edges, about 5 minutes. Increase the heat to medium-high and cook without stirring until the syrup is a golden color and hits the caramel stage on a candy thermometer (340°F/170°C), about 10 minutes.

Remove the caramel from the heat and stir in the baking soda and ¼ tsp of the salt with a heat-resistant spatula. Stir in the chopped peanuts, then pour the caramel onto the prepared baking sheet. Cool completely to room temperature to form a peanut brittle.

Pulse the peanut brittle in a food processor for a few seconds to break it up. Add the peanut butter, the remaining 2 tsp of vanilla extract, and the remaining ¼ tsp of salt, grinding the mixture to a dough that has a mixture of textured bits of brittle and finely ground peanut brittle, 15–30 seconds.

Line a baking sheet with parchment paper. In a double boiler, very carefully melt the chocolate. Using an offset spatula, spread a layer of the chocolate onto the prepared baking sheet and refrigerate until firm.

When firm, add the peanut butter brittle filling and spread to the edges. Finally, add the remaining chocolate and spread with offset spatula to cover the filling. Sprinkle with the extra chopped peanuts and refrigerate until firm, about 30 minutes. It can stay refrigerated until you're ready to decorate the cake.

Determine how much peanut butter cup crunch you want to add to your cake, cut off that size of chunk and chop it up into small irregular pieces. Slice the remaining slab into bars to keep in an airtight container in the fridge for up to 2 weeks and eat whenever the mood strikes.

ASSEMBLE THE CAKE

Follow the steps on pages 19–22 to fill and frost the cake using the strawberry jam and peanut butter Swiss meringue buttercream, to the final frost stage. While building the cake layers, follow the jam dam or dugout pool method to carve out a small pool in the center of the buttercream and add some jam to the layers. For the photo opposite, I used an au naturel style for the second layer of frosting, using an offset spatula to create swoops in the frosting.

Add your desired design elements to the frosted cake: try a piped shell border, or some piped drop stars, to your liking. Top the cake with a glorious heap of peanut butter cup crunch, and some extra strawberries for color and flavor.

This cake will taste freshest eaten within a day of making it, but can be stored in the fridge, covered, for up to 3 days. See page 13 for storage notes.

Cake

2½ cups (350g) all-purpose flour

2 cups (400g) granulated white sugar

1 cup (120g) Dutch-process cocoa powder

2½ tsp baking soda

1¼ tsp baking powder

1 tsp sea salt

2¼ cups (560ml) full-fat coconut milk

½ cup (125ml) vegetable oil

2 tsp apple cider vinegar

2 tsp pure vanilla extract

Filling + Frosting

1 recipe Chocolate Ganache Frosting (page 139)

Rainbow sprinkles (optional)

Fresh raspberry (optional)

EASY CHOCOLATE CAKE WITH CHOCOLATE GANACHE FROSTING

MAKES ONE 7-INCH 3-LAYER CAKE

This is a variation of one of my favorite chocolate cakes I've been making for over a decade—moist, chocolaty, and tender, paired with rich and lustrous chocolate ganache. Frost gently, as if you're handling a tiny fluffy bunny, as it has a tender chocolate crumb. I like to finish this cake with creamy swoops in the frosting using my offset spatula, but you can also add any of your favorite finishing touches—sprinkles, fresh berries, or chocolate shards.

MAKE THE CAKE

Preheat the oven to 350°F (175°C). Prepare three 7- × 2-inch round cake pans by spritzing them with vegetable oil and lining with parchment paper circles cut to size, and then spritzing again with oil, to prevent sticking.

In the bowl of a stand mixer fitted with the paddle attachment, mix together the flour, sugar, cocoa powder, baking soda, baking powder, and salt on low speed until combined.

In a large bowl, whisk together the coconut milk, vegetable oil, apple cider vinegar, and vanilla extract.

With the mixer on low speed, pour in the coconut milk mixture and mix to combine, no more than 30 seconds. If needed, finish the batter by hand using a rubber spatula so it's smooth and lump-free.

BAKE THE CAKE

Divide the batter evenly between the prepared cake pans. Tap each pan gently on the counter to reduce any air bubbles. Bake for 22–25 minutes, until a toothpick inserted into the center of the cake comes out with only moist crumbs.

Let the cakes cool completely in their pans set on top of wire racks.

ASSEMBLE THE CAKE

Follow the steps on pages 19–22 to fill and frost the cake using the chocolate ganache frosting, to the final frost stage. For the photo opposite, I used a combo of smooth and au naturel styles for my second layer of frosting, using an offset spatula to create swoops in the frosting on top. Finish your cake with sprinkles and a fresh raspberry (it's also delicious with just a sprinkling of flaky sea salt).

This cake will taste freshest eaten within a day of making it, but can be stored in the fridge, covered, for up to 3 days. See page 13 for storage notes.

Chocolate Cake

1 cup (250ml) soy milk

2 tsp apple cider vinegar

1 cup (250ml) hot coffee

¾ cup (90g) Dutch-process cocoa powder

½ cup (125ml) vegetable oil

2 tsp pure vanilla extract

2 cups (280g) all-purpose flour

2 cups (400g) granulated white sugar

1 tsp baking powder

1 tsp baking soda

1 tsp fine sea salt

Filling + Frosting

Raspberry jam (page 141) or use your favorite store-bought

1 recipe Vanilla Swiss Meringue Buttercream (page 130)

Pink and turquoise gel colors (or colors of your choice)

Fresh raspberries

PARTY TIME CHOCOLATE RASPBERRY RUFFLE CAKE

MAKES ONE 7-INCH 3-LAYER CAKE

A cake walks into a room and says . . . "party time!" Tough to get more charming than this pink-and-turquoise, ruffly cartoon-looking chocolate cake with vanilla Swiss meringue buttercream. I've fancied the cake up with vintage-piped ruffles and fresh raspberries in a pop of color, but you could also try it with any number of piping styles, or keep it simple with just a piped border, raspberries, and sprinkles.

MAKE THE CAKE

Preheat the oven to 350°F (175°C). Prepare three 7- × 2-inch round cake pans by spritzing them with vegetable oil and lining with parchment paper circles cut to size, and then spritzing again with oil, to prevent sticking.

In a small bowl, mix the soy milk with the apple cider vinegar and set aside for 10 minutes to thicken. It may look a bit separated at this point, but that's normal.

In a medium bowl, whisk together the hot coffee and cocoa powder into a coffee slurry. Add the soy milk mixture, vegetable oil, and vanilla extract, whisking to combine.

In the bowl of a stand mixer fitted with the paddle attachment, mix together the flour, sugar, baking powder, baking soda, and salt. With the mixer on low speed, slowly add the hot coffee mixture, mixing until combined and a smooth batter forms, about 30 seconds.

BAKE THE CAKE

Pour the batter into the prepared cake pans, giving them a light tap on the counter to reduce any air bubbles. Bake for 30–34 minutes, until a toothpick inserted into the center of the cake comes out with only moist crumbs, and cake feels springy to the touch.

Let the cakes cool completely in their pans set on top of wire racks.

continued

ASSEMBLE THE CAKE

Scoop 1 cup (250ml) of the buttercream into a separate bowl and tint it with just a touch of pink gel color. Tint the remaining buttercream a light turquoise.

Follow the steps on pages 19–22 to fill and frost the cake with the raspberry jam and light turquoise buttercream. Add the jam to each layer using either the jam dam or dugout pool method. Place fresh raspberries on top of the first layer of buttercream, pushing them into the frosting, and then add a thin layer of additional frosting on top of the raspberries, using an offset spatula to cover the berries with the buttercream. Add the second layer of cake and repeat with the jam, buttercream, and raspberries. Frost the cake to the final frost stage, making sure to reserve at least ½ cup of the turquoise buttercream for the next step.

Tint the remaining turquoise buttercream darker by adding a little more gel color. Fit a piping bag with a large leaf tip and fill the bag with the darker turquoise buttercream. Fit a second piping bag with a 1M open star tip and fill that bag with the pink buttercream.

Pipe a turquoise ruffle border along the bottom of the cake, and pipe a pink shell border on top of it. Then pipe a turquoise swag design around the cake (read more on page 28), marking with a toothpick your start and end points to make it even. Add another pink shell border to the top edge of the cake, and another ruffle border on top of the cake. Decorate with fresh raspberries!

This cake will taste freshest eaten within a day of making it, but can be stored in the fridge, covered, for up to 3 days. See page 13 for storage notes.

Cake

3 cups (420g) all-purpose flour

2 cups (400g) granulated white sugar

2 tsp baking soda

1 tsp salt

1½ cups (375ml) boiling water

1 tbsp instant espresso granules

⅔ cup (80g) Dutch-process cocoa powder

1 cup (250ml) vegetable oil

1 tbsp pure vanilla extract

¼ cup (60ml) apple cider vinegar

Chocolate Hazelnut Filling

1½ cups (200g) toasted hazelnuts (without skin)

1 tsp pure vanilla extract

2 tbsp granulated white sugar + more to taste

½ tsp fine sea salt

½ cup (90g) semisweet or dark plant-based chocolate (not unsweetened), chopped, melted, and cooled

Candied Hazelnuts

¾ cup (150g) granulated white sugar

3 tbsp water

1 cup (135g) toasted hazelnuts (without skin)

Flaky sea salt

Frosting

1 recipe Chocolate Swiss Meringue Buttercream (page 131)

CHOCOLATE HAZELNUT CAKE WITH CANDIED HAZELNUTS

MAKES ONE 7-INCH 3-LAYER CAKE

Good old chocolate and hazelnut is one of my husband Rich's favorite flavor combinations. This cake—a toasty, chocolaty, nutty, creamy delight—has a homemade chocolate hazelnut filling that is as easy to prepare as it is delicious and is topped with candied hazelnuts that give a perfect sweet and salty crunch (ideal for those nut-lovin' nuts in your life). I use Chocolate Swiss Meringue Buttercream (page 131) as the frosting, but you could use any of the chocolate frostings in the book, such as the Chocolate Fudge Buttercream on page 126.

 Leftover chocolate hazelnut filling can be eaten by the spoonful or slathered on the nearest piece of toast. If you're not feeling in the mood to make your own filling, store-bought plant-based chocolate hazelnut filling works great too.

MAKE THE CAKE

Preheat the oven to 350°F (175°C). Prepare three 7- × 2-inch round cake pans by spritzing them with vegetable oil and lining with parchment paper circles cut to size, and then spritzing again with oil, to prevent sticking.

In the bowl of a stand mixer fitted with the whisk attachment, whisk the flour, sugar, baking soda, and salt until combined. With the machine turned off, switch to the paddle attachment.

In a large bowl, combine the boiling water and espresso powder and whisk to combine. Whisk in the cocoa powder until combined. Whisk in the vegetable oil and vanilla extract (don't worry if it won't emulsify, it will all come together!).

continued

PARTY ANIMAL THREE-LAYER CAKES

Add this wet mixture to the bowl of the stand mixer and mix on low speed for about 20 seconds to combine. Add the apple cider vinegar and mix until combined and the batter is smooth, about another 15 seconds, using a spatula to scrape down the sides of the bowl if needed.

BAKE THE CAKE

Divide the batter evenly between the prepared cake pans. Give the pans a light tap on the counter to reduce any air bubbles. Bake for 22–25 minutes, until the cake springs back to the touch, and a toothpick inserted in the center comes back with only moist crumbs.

Let the cakes cool completely in their pans set on top of wire racks.

MAKE THE CHOCOLATE HAZELNUT FILLING

Using a food processor, blitz the toasted hazelnuts until smooth and creamy, essentially making them into a nut butter. Add the vanilla extract, the 2 tbsp of sugar, and salt and give it another little blend. Slowly stream in the melted slightly cooled chocolate, a little at a time, blending until fully incorporated. Add more sugar, 1 tsp at a time, until you reach your desired sweetness. Store the chocolate hazelnut filling in an airtight container in the fridge for up to 1 week.

MAKE THE CANDIED HAZELNUTS

Line a baking sheet with parchment paper and set aside.

In a small saucepan set over high heat, heat the sugar and water until the sugar dissolves. Bring to a simmer, swirling the pan occasionally, until the mixture is medium amber in color, about 4 minutes. Add the hazelnuts and stir to combine.

Immediately pour the candied nuts onto the prepared baking sheet, spreading them out evenly. Sprinkle with flaky sea salt before the candy hardens. Let cool completely, then break up into shards and small pieces for inserting into the top of the cake. Store the candied nuts in an airtight container at room temperature for up to 3 days.

ASSEMBLE THE CAKE

Follow the steps on pages 19–22 to fill and frost the cake to the final frost stage using the chocolate hazelnut filling and chocolate Swiss meringue buttercream. While building the cake layers, follow the dugout pool method to carve out a small pool in the center of the buttercream and add some chocolate hazelnut filling to the layers. Alternately, you can pipe a buttercream dam around the edge of your cake (see page 19). For the photo opposite, I used an au naturel style for the second layer of frosting to keep it rustic looking with swoops of frosting (see page 22).

Once frosted, artfully arrange various sizes of candied hazelnut shards into the buttercream on the top of the cake.

This cake will taste freshest eaten within a day of making it, but can be stored in the fridge, covered, for up to 3 days. See page 13 for storage notes.

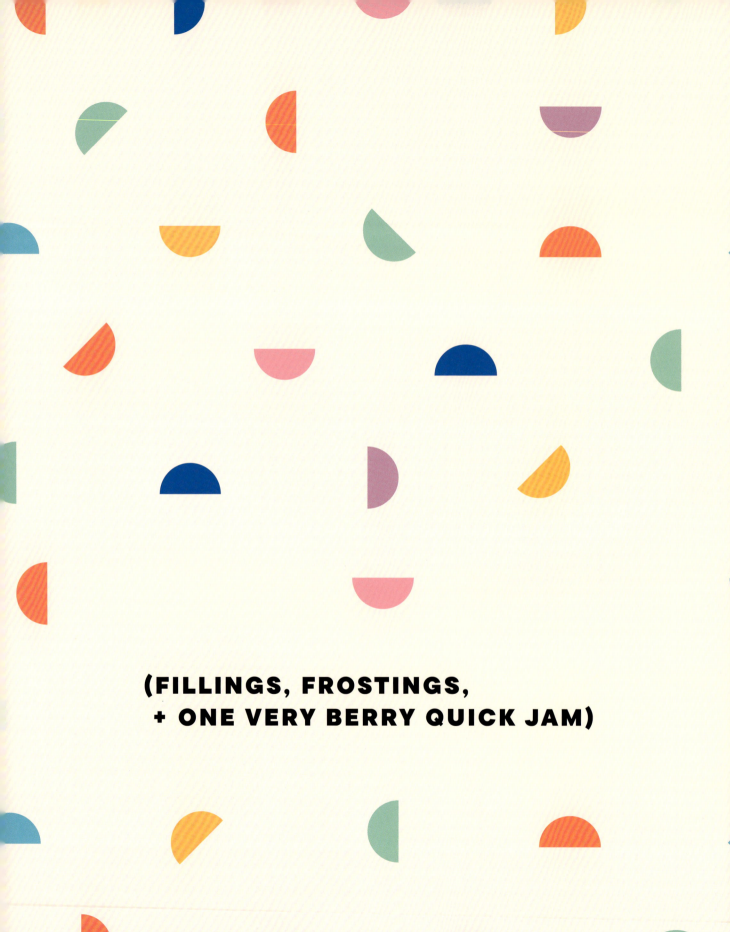

(FILLINGS, FROSTINGS,
+ ONE VERY BERRY QUICK JAM)

4

BUTTERCREAM DREAMS

BUTTERCREAM DREAMS

Classic buttercreams, Swiss meringue buttercream, Italian meringue buttercream—whatever you fancy, we can make it plants-y! Here we dive in to all of the frostings in *Plantcakes*; get ready to bathe in frosting!

CLASSIC BUTTERCREAM
Ah, buttercream. Many of us started our cake journeys by whipping up a simple classic buttercream. With its minimal ingredients—butter, icing sugar, and flavoring—it's easy, creamy, and delicious, perfect for kids' parties, or a fast, simple frosting for snacking cakes.

SWISS MERINGUE BUTTERCREAM
Meringue-based buttercreams are smooth and silky, and a cake frosted with one tastes like a little creamy dreamy slice o' heaven. It takes a little more effort to make than a classic buttercream, but once you get used to making it, it becomes second nature!

A meringue buttercream starts with—you guessed it—meringue! For plant-based baking, that means making meringue using our protein-packed, viscous, egg-white-like friend aquafaba (i.e., the liquid in a can of chickpeas; read more on page 8). I first learned about making aquafaba meringue–based buttercreams through the fantastic website Gretchen's Vegan Bakery: www.gretchensveganbakery.com. Gretchen is an early innovator in vegan baking and an inspiration to many. Once you have your whipped meringue, you then add sugar, butter, and flavorings, and it all whips into a creamy, not-too-sweet, silky smooth buttercream.

As an alternative to aquafaba, you can also use a soy-based powder called Versawhip. Versawhip is a molecular gastronomy discovery, most often used to make fancy foams for restaurants. Add water to the Versawhip powder, and it miraculously whips up into a meringue, providing a stable (and vegan!) meringue base for buttercreams (read more on page 130).

ITALIAN MERINGUE BUTTERCREAM
Italian meringue buttercreams also have a meringue base, but rather than adding sugar, you pour a hot sugar syrup into the whipped meringue. The sugar syrup needs to reach 240°F (115°C)—also known as the "soft ball" stage—which you can measure with a candy thermometer. Sometimes folks get a little wary when recipes call for things like "hot sugar syrup" and "candy thermometers," but if you've made any type of candy or brittle before on the stovetop, a little hot sugar syrup shouldn't be too frightening!

FINDING YOUR FAVORITE FATS
I've experimented with several of the plant-based butters and vegetable shortenings available in North America, and when it comes down to picking the right one, it's all about the holy trinity of flavor, mouthfeel, and stability. Think about which aspects are most important to you and find your favorite balance through experimenting!

Plant-Based Butter
All the recipes in this book call for unsalted plant butter. I personally recommend the brick form of Becel unsalted butter or Flora unsalted butter.

While I love the flavor of Miyoko's Creamery organic butter, I find Becel and Flora to be the most stable commercial varieties that won't be melty at room temperature (see below). Note that the butter sold in bricks is different from the spreads found in tubs; spreads have a higher water content, so are not recommended for making buttercream. Your local grocery chain may make their own plant-based brick butter, so feel free to experiment with it, but Becel and Flora are very readily available and the brands I always return to.

TO SALT OR NOT TO SALT: Use unsalted butter if you can. It's nice to be able to control the saltiness of the buttercream—hence, the recipes in this book call for unsalted butter, with a pinch of salt added. Not to worry if you only have salted butter—just don't add the salt called for in the recipe.

THE GREAT MIND MELT: When making buttercream, make sure your butter is at room temperature (for meringue buttercreams, you want the meringue and butter to be at roughly the same temperature to meld into a lovely whipped buttercream), otherwise your buttercream may split or curdle. Keep in mind that some plant-based butters will be more melty at room temperature, so those should be used more promptly after coming to room temperature, or even soon after removing from the fridge. You can do a simple test for this: slice off a little piece of butter and put it on a plate; if it's liquid or melty after an hour or so out, then this butter is one that should be used promptly from the fridge rather than at room temperature.

If your butter is prone to melting, keep your cake refrigerated throughout the frosting process, and keep it refrigerated until shortly before serving too. A melting buttercream is a sad and frustrating buttercream for any baker, even if it still tastes amazing! Sometimes if I'm sensing a potentially melty butter situation, I implement this mantra, just to avoid any disappointment: "You gotta keep it refrigerated" (sung to the tune of The Offspring, hehe).

Veggie Shortening—Friend or Foe?
Only one recipe in this book—my Supermarket Bakery–Style Cake with Pink Vanilla Buttercream (page 75)—calls for vegetable shortening, but some bakers swear by mixing vegetable shortening with their butter, as it helps add stability to the buttercream (or to mimic the nostalgic consistency of a supermarket bakery cake, which I love!). Some folks dislike the mouthfeel of vegetable shortening in buttercream, but I find the combination of plant-based butter and vegetable shortening can be your friend. Generally, vegetable shortening has very little flavor. You may decide a mixture of butter and vegetable shortening works best for you, such as half plant-based butter and half vegetable shortening, or three-quarters plant-based butter and one-quarter shortening. Experiment with your favorite combinations and always keep in mind that holy trinity of plant-based buttercream: flavor, mouthfeel, and stability (should this be my new tattoo?).

The best vegetable shortening I've used is Spectrum high-ratio organic vegetable shortening. I find it to be traceless when used in either meringue or classic buttercreams. More commercially available varieties, such as Crisco, can work well too.

TROUBLESHOOTING MERINGUE BUTTERCREAM
Sometimes bakers run into trouble with meringue-based buttercreams—soupy, won't thicken, separates—when your buttercream gets bratty, look to these methods to help out!

SOUPY BUTTERCREAM: This means your buttercream has gotten too warm. If your buttercream becomes a big old liquid soup, give it a quick chill in the fridge for 5 to 10 minutes, then beat it again until a thick buttercream forms. Repeat if necessary.

CURDLED OR SPLIT BUTTERCREAM: This means your buttercream had a too-cold element to it, such as too-cold butter, that "broke" the buttercream. Try heating it up in a stainless-steel mixing bowl for 15 seconds on the stovetop until it looks a bit melty around the sides. (I turn on my gas stovetop range and hold it over the flame for 5–10 seconds. If you have a kitchen blowtorch, you can try that too.) Beat it again until a thick buttercream forms. Repeat if necessary. If you have a microwave, you could microwave a small portion of the buttercream (half a cup) and then add that back to the main mixture, beating again until a thick buttercream forms. Repeat if necessary.

MELTY BUTTERCREAM: A non-room-temperature-stable butter was probably the culprit here (read more on page 122). Just keep your buttercream refrigerated until frosting and also during frosting, and then keep the frosted cake refrigerated until serving!

CLASSIC BUTTERCREAMS

VANILLA BUTTERCREAM

MAKES ENOUGH FOR 1 LARGE CAKE OR 24 CUPCAKES

- 2 cups (454g) unsalted plant-based butter, room temperature
- 3 cups (390g) icing sugar, sifted (see note)
- 2 tsp pure vanilla extract
- Pinch of salt + more to taste

In the bowl of a stand mixer fitted with the paddle attachment, beat the butter on high speed until doubled in volume, about 1 minute, using a spatula to scrape down the sides of the bowl as needed.

With the mixer turned off, add the icing sugar, vanilla extract, and salt. Pulse on low speed to gently combine without causing a dust storm. Once combined, increase to high speed and beat until the frosting is fluffy and creamy, another 1–2 minutes.

Store any leftover buttercream in an airtight container in the fridge for up to 1 week.

> **NOTE:** If making this buttercream for cupcakes, like the Garden Party Vanilla Lemon Cupcakes (page 210) or Chocolate Chip Cupcakes (page 215), add an extra ½ cup (65g) icing sugar to make the buttercream stiffer and easier to pipe.

VANILLA BEAN BUTTERCREAM

MAKES ENOUGH FOR 1 LARGE CAKE OR 24 CUPCAKES

- 2 cups (454g) unsalted plant-based butter, room temperature
- 4 cups (520g) icing sugar, sifted
- 2 tsp pure vanilla extract
- 1 tsp vanilla bean paste, or seeds from 1 vanilla bean
- Pinch of salt + more to taste

Follow the method for Vanilla Buttercream on this page, adding the vanilla bean paste with the vanilla extract.

CHOCOLATE BUTTERCREAM

MAKES ENOUGH FOR 1 LARGE CAKE OR 24 CUPCAKES

- 2 cups (454g) unsalted plant-based butter, room temperature
- 3 cups (390g) icing sugar, sifted
- ¾ cup (90g) Dutch-process cocoa powder
- 2 tsp pure vanilla extract
- Pinch of salt + more to taste

Follow the method for Vanilla Buttercream on this page, adding the cocoa powder with the icing sugar.

CHOCOLATE FUDGE BUTTERCREAM

MAKES ENOUGH FOR 1 LARGE CAKE OR 24 CUPCAKES

- ¾ cup (170g) chopped dark or bittersweet plant-based chocolate
- 1 cup (224g) unsalted plant-based butter, room temperature
- 2 cups (260g) icing sugar, sifted
- ¼ cup (30g) Dutch-process cocoa powder
- 1 tsp pure vanilla extract
- 2 tbsp plant milk + more as needed
- Pinch of salt + more to taste

Using a double boiler or a glass bowl set atop a small saucepan filled a quarter full of water, heat the chocolate over medium-high heat until melted. Remove from the heat and set aside to cool.

In the bowl of a stand mixer fitted with the paddle attachment, pulse the butter, icing sugar, cocoa powder, vanilla extract, and cooled chocolate on low speed a few times to combine the ingredients without causing a dust storm. Once combined, turn the mixer to low and add the plant milk and salt. Turn the mixer to medium speed and beat until everything is incorporated, using a spatula to scrape down the sides of the bowl as needed, and then whip on high speed to fluff it up into a creamy frosting, about 1 minute. If the frosting seems too stiff, add about another 1 tbsp of plant milk.

SALTED CARAMEL BUTTERCREAM

MAKES ENOUGH FOR 1 LARGE CAKE OR 24 CUPCAKES

Salted Caramel
- 1 cup (200g) granulated white sugar
- 2 tbsp corn syrup
- 2 tbsp water
- ½ cup (125ml) plant milk
- 2 tbsp unsalted plant-based butter
- 1 tsp pure vanilla extract
- 1 tsp fine sea salt

Salted Caramel Buttercream
- 1¾ cups (392g) unsalted plant-based butter, room temperature
- 2 cups (260g) icing sugar, sifted + more as needed
- 2 tsp pure vanilla extract

MAKE THE SALTED CARAMEL

In a heavy-bottomed saucepan, melt the sugar, corn syrup, and water over high heat until the sugar has dissolved. Let the mixture boil without stirring until it reaches a medium amber color, about 10 minutes or so. Remove from the heat and carefully whisk in the plant milk (it will bubble up ferociously, so go slowly). Whisk in the butter, vanilla extract, and salt. Let cool completely; it will thicken as it cools.

Use ¾ cup (185ml) salted caramel for the buttercream (below), and reserve the rest for decorating the cake with caramel drips. Leftover caramel will keep in the fridge for up to 2 weeks—it is delicious drizzled on ice cream or stirred into yogurt.

MAKE THE SALTED CARAMEL BUTTERCREAM

In the bowl of a stand mixer fitted with the paddle attachment, beat the butter, icing sugar, vanilla extract, and ¾ cup (185ml) of the salted caramel on low speed to combine, using a spatula to scrape down the sides of the bowl as needed. Turn the mixer to medium-high speed and beat until light and fluffy, about 1 minute. If the frosting seems too loose, add 1 tbsp of icing sugar at a time to thicken it until it is creamy and spreadable, being careful not to over-sweeten.

PEANUT BUTTER FROSTING

MAKES ENOUGH FOR 1 LARGE CAKE OR 24 CUPCAKES

1½ cups (340g) unsalted plant-based butter, room temperature

½ cup (125g) smooth peanut butter (see note on page 62)

3 cups (390g) icing sugar, sifted

2 tsp pure vanilla extract

Pinch of salt + more to taste

In the bowl of a stand mixer fitted with the paddle attachment, beat the butter on high speed until doubled in volume, about 1 minute, using a spatula to scrape down the sides of the bowl as needed. With the mixer turned off, add the peanut butter, icing sugar, vanilla extract, and salt and pulse on low speed to combine. Beat the mixture on medium speed until thickened and incorporated, about 1 minute.

STRAWBERRY BUTTERCREAM

MAKES ENOUGH FOR 1 LARGE CAKE OR 24 CUPCAKES

¼ cup (30g) freeze-dried strawberries

2 cups (454g) unsalted plant-based butter, room temperature

3½ cups (455g) icing sugar, sifted

2 tsp pure vanilla extract

Pinch of salt + more to taste

In a food processor, blitz the freeze-dried strawberries into a fine powder.

In the bowl of a stand mixer fitted with the paddle attachment, beat the butter, icing sugar, vanilla extract, salt, and strawberry powder on low speed to combine. Increase the speed to medium-high, beating until light and fluffy, about 1 minute.

COTTON CANDY BUTTERCREAM

MAKES ENOUGH FOR 1 LARGE CAKE OR 24 CUPCAKES

2 cups (454g) unsalted plant-based butter, room temperature

3 cups (390g) icing sugar, sifted

1 tbsp cotton candy extract

1 tsp pure vanilla extract

Pinch of salt + more to taste

Follow the method for the Vanilla Buttercream on page 125, adding the cotton candy extract along with the vanilla extract and salt.

PINK VANILLA FROSTING

MAKES ENOUGH FOR 1 LARGE CAKE OR 24 CUPCAKES

1 cup (224g) unsalted plant-based butter, room temperature

½ cup (103g) vegetable shortening

2 cups (260g) icing sugar, sifted

2 tsp pure vanilla extract

1 tsp pink natural food coloring powder or ⅛ tsp pink gel color

Pinch of salt + more to taste

In the bowl of a stand mixer fitted with the paddle attachment, beat the butter and vegetable shortening on medium-high speed until doubled in volume, about 1 minute, using a spatula to scrape down the sides of the bowl as needed.

With the mixer off, add the icing sugar, vanilla extract, pink natural food coloring powder or pink gel color, and salt. Pulse on low speed to gently combine without causing a dust storm. Once combined, increase the speed to high and mix until the frosting is fluffy, creamy, and pink, about another minute.

SWISS MERINGUE BUTTERCREAMS

Creamy dreamy SMBC! Here are my Swiss meringue-based buttercream recipes, with two options for making the plant-based meringue they use as their base: aquafaba and Versawhip. Before you begin whipping either of them, make sure your stand mixer's bowl and whisk attachment are completely grease-free—to do this, rub the inside of the bowl and the whisk with half of a lemon, then dry them to make sure there's no grease whatsoever. Whipping meringue requires a powerful machine to do the job—a stand mixer fitted with a whisk attachment is perfect—and note that it may take a long time, sometimes almost 15 minutes. (Use this whipping time to multitask . . . wash dishes, make a ganache, listen to a podcast!) If you find your meringue just won't get to stiff peaks, don't panic—I've made many buttercreams with my meringue not being perfectly stiff.

AQUAFABA MERINGUE FOR SWISS MERINGUE BUTTERCREAM
MAKES ABOUT 5 CUPS

For aquafaba meringue, I like to reduce the aquafaba on the stovetop first to concentrate or thicken it, adding sugar once it has reduced, to make something akin to an aquafaba syrup. After removing from it the stovetop, I let this mixture cool down on the counter, then I refrigerate it overnight, or for at least a few hours, which allows it to thicken into a gelatinous consistency. This isn't an essential step, but it's the method I've had most consistently good results with, so I recommend trying it for sure. The prepared aquafaba will start as a golden color, then as it froths and whips, it will turn into a fluffy white meringue. Once the aquafaba has fluffed up to the soft peaks stage, you start adding the icing sugar mixed with cream of tartar in 1 tbsp increments—cream of tartar is aquafaba's best little buddy, helping it stabilize and stay whipped.

- 2 cans (18 oz/540ml each) unsalted chickpeas
- 1 cup (200g) granulated white sugar
- 1 cup (130g) icing sugar, sifted
- ½ tsp cream of tartar

NOTE: The reduced aquafaba needs at least 2 hours to chill, and ideally overnight to jell, so start this meringue preparation ahead of time. It can be prepared up to 5 days in advance and stored in the fridge until needed.

SEPARATE THE AQUAFABA
Pour the chickpeas and their liquid into a strainer set over a medium bowl, straining the aquafaba liquid into the bowl. Reserve the chickpeas for another use.

REDUCE THE AQUAFABA
Transfer the aquafaba liquid to a small saucepan set over medium-high heat. Bring the aquafaba to a low boil (watching that it doesn't boil over), then turn the heat down to low. Simmer the aquafaba until it is reduced by approximately half—you want to end up with roughly 1 cup (250ml) of reduced aquafaba—this could take up to 15 minutes.

Once the aquafaba has reduced, remove the saucepan from the heat and add the white sugar, whisking to combine.

continued

BUTTERCREAM DREAMS

CHILL THE AQUAFABA

Transfer the aquafaba to a heatproof liquid measuring cup or container. Refrigerate, covered, for at least 2 hours and ideally overnight to jell. When reduced aquafaba is refrigerated, it takes on a thick gelatinous consistency. It will be a golden color and it may separate a bit, and all of this is normal.

WHIP THE CHILLED AQUAFABA

In the bowl of a stand mixer fitted with the whisk attachment, beat the chilled aquafaba on low speed for 3 minutes. Increase the speed to medium-high and whip for 3 more minutes.

In a small bowl, sift the icing sugar and cream of tartar together. Add the mixture to the stand mixer, 1 tbsp at a time, and continue whipping until the meringue has thickened into glossy, firm peaks. This may take up to 15 minutes. Leave the meringue in the bowl of the stand mixer, and continue with the method of the buttercream recipe you're using.

VERSAWHIP MERINGUE FOR SWISS MERINGUE BUTTERCREAM

MAKES ABOUT 5 CUPS

- 1½ tsp dry Versawhip powder
- ¾ cup (185ml) warm water
- 1 cup (130g) icing sugar
- ½ tsp cream of tartar
- 1 cup (200g) granulated white sugar

In a liquid measuring cup, whisk the dry Versawhip powder with the warm water to dissolve.

In a small bowl, sift the icing sugar and cream of tartar together and set aside.

In the bowl of a stand mixer fitted with the whisk attachment, whisk the Versawhip mixture on low speed for 2 minutes to begin the formation of meringue. Increase the speed to high and slowly add the white sugar, 1 tbsp at a time. Then add the icing sugar mixture, 1 tbsp at a time. Continue whipping at high speed until stiff peaks are achieved, about 5–8 minutes. Leave this meringue in the bowl of the stand mixer, and continue with the method of the buttercream recipe you're using.

VANILLA SWISS MERINGUE BUTTERCREAM

MAKES ENOUGH FOR 1 LARGE CAKE OR 24 CUPCAKES

- 1 recipe Aquafaba Meringue for Swiss Meringue Buttercream (page 129) or 1 recipe Versawhip Meringue for Swiss Meringue Buttercream (this page)
- 2 cups (454g) unsalted plant-based butter, room temperature
- 2 tsp pure vanilla extract
- ½ tsp vanilla bean paste
- Pinch of salt + more to taste

With the meringue in the bowl of the stand mixer, switch to the paddle attachment. With the mixer on low speed, add the butter; I use a butter knife and just slice off small pieces of butter right into the mixer. Whip on high speed until a glossy, silky frosting forms, about 1 minute.

Add the vanilla extract, vanilla paste, and salt and whip for another 30 seconds to combine, using a spatula to scrape down the sides of the bowl as needed. If you run into any trouble, see "Troubleshooting Meringue Buttercream" on page 122.

Store any leftover buttercream in an airtight container in the fridge for up to 1 week.

CHOCOLATE SWISS MERINGUE BUTTERCREAM

MAKES ENOUGH FOR 1 LARGE CAKE OR 24 CUPCAKES

- 1 recipe Aquafaba Meringue for Swiss Meringue Buttercream (page 129) or 1 recipe Versawhip Meringue for Swiss Meringue Buttercream (page 130)
- 2 cups (454g) unsalted plant-based butter, room temperature
- 1 tsp pure vanilla extract
- Pinch of salt
- ½ cup (90g) chopped plant-based chocolate

Using a double boiler or a glass bowl set atop a small saucepan filled a quarter full of water, heat the chocolate over medium-low heat until melted. Remove from the heat and set aside to cool.

Follow the method for the Vanilla Swiss Meringue Buttercream on page 130. Add the melted, cooled chocolate at the end, whipping for another 15–30 seconds to combine, using a spatula to scrape down the sides of the bowl as needed.

COFFEE SWISS MERINGUE BUTTERCREAM

MAKES ENOUGH FOR 1 LARGE CAKE OR 24 CUPCAKES

- ½ tsp instant coffee granules
- ¼ cup (60ml) plant milk
- 1 recipe Aquafaba Meringue for Swiss Meringue Buttercream (page 129) or 1 recipe Versawhip Meringue for Swiss Meringue Buttercream (page 130)
- 2 cups (454g) unsalted plant-based butter, room temperature
- 2 tsp pure vanilla extract
- 1 tsp coffee-flavored extract
- Pinch of salt

In a small cup, dissolve the instant coffee granules in the soy milk and set aside.

Follow the method for the Vanilla Swiss Meringue Buttercream on page 130, adding the coffee milk and coffee extract with the vanilla extract and salt and whipping for another minute to combine. Use a spatula to scrape down the sides of the bowl as needed.

PEANUT BUTTER SWISS MERINGUE BUTTERCREAM

MAKES ENOUGH FOR 1 LARGE CAKE OR 24 CUPCAKES

- 1 recipe Aquafaba Meringue for Swiss Meringue Buttercream (page 129) or 1 recipe Versawhip Meringue for Swiss Meringue Buttercream (page 130)
- 2 cups (454g) unsalted plant-based butter, room temperature
- 1 cup (250g) smooth commercial brand peanut butter
- 1 tsp pure vanilla extract
- Pinch of salt

Follow the method for the Vanilla Swiss Meringue Buttercream on page 130, adding the peanut butter along with the vanilla extract and salt. Whip for another minute to combine, using a spatula to scrape down the sides of the bowl as needed.

RASPBERRY SWISS MERINGUE BUTTERCREAM

MAKES ENOUGH FOR 1 LARGE CAKE OR 24 CUPCAKES

- 1 recipe Aquafaba Meringue for Swiss Meringue Buttercream (page 129) or 1 recipe Versawhip Meringue for Swiss Meringue Buttercream (page 130)
- 2 cups (454g) unsalted plant-based butter, room temperature
- 2 tsp pure vanilla extract
- ½ tsp vanilla bean paste
- ½ cup (30g) freeze-dried raspberries, powdered
- Pinch of salt

Follow the method for the Vanilla Swiss Meringue Buttercream on page 130, adding the powdered freeze-dried raspberries along with the vanilla extract, vanilla bean paste, and salt. Mix on medium-high speed for another minute to combine, using a spatula to scrape down the sides of the bowl as needed.

STRAWBERRY SWISS MERINGUE BUTTERCREAM

MAKES ENOUGH FOR 1 LARGE CAKE OR 24 CUPCAKES

- 1 recipe Aquafaba Meringue for Swiss Meringue Buttercream (page 129) or 1 recipe Versawhip Meringue for Swiss Meringue Buttercream (page 130)
- 2 cups (454g) unsalted plant-based butter, room temperature
- ½ cup (30g) freeze-dried strawberries, powdered
- Pinch of salt

Follow the method for the Vanilla Swiss Meringue Buttercream on page 130, adding the powdered freeze-dried strawberries and salt after the butter. Mix for another minute to combine, using a spatula to scrape down the sides of the bowl as needed.

LEMON SWISS MERINGUE BUTTERCREAM

MAKES ENOUGH FOR 1 LARGE CAKE OR 24 CUPCAKES

- 1 recipe Aquafaba Meringue for Swiss Meringue Buttercream (page 129) or 1 recipe Versawhip Meringue for Swiss Meringue Buttercream (page 130)
- 2 cups (454g) unsalted plant-based butter, room temperature
- ½ cup (125ml) fresh squeezed lemon juice
- 1 tbsp lemon zest
- Pinch of salt

Follow the method for the Vanilla Swiss Meringue Buttercream on page 130, adding the lemon juice, lemon zest, and salt after the butter. Mix to combine for about 1 minute, using a spatula to scrape down the sides of the bowl as needed.

PASSION FRUIT VANILLA SWISS MERINGUE BUTTERCREAM

MAKES ENOUGH FOR 1 LARGE CAKE OR 24 CUPCAKES

- 1 recipe Aquafaba Meringue for Swiss Meringue Buttercream (page 129) or 1 recipe Versawhip Meringue for Swiss Meringue Buttercream (page 130)
- 2 cups (454g) unsalted plant-based butter, room temperature
- 1 cup (200g) granulated white sugar
- 2 tbsp vanilla bean paste
- ½ cup (30g) freeze-dried powdered passion fruit
- Pinch of salt

Follow the method for the Vanilla Swiss Meringue Buttercream on page 130, adding the vanilla bean paste, powdered freeze-dried passion fruit, and salt after the butter. Mix to combine for about 1 minute, using a spatula to scrape down the sides of the bowl as needed.

COCONUT SWISS MERINGUE BUTTERCREAM

MAKES ENOUGH FOR 1 LARGE CAKE OR 24 CUPCAKES

- 1 recipe Aquafaba Meringue for Swiss Meringue Buttercream (page 129) or 1 recipe Versawhip Meringue for Swiss Meringue Buttercream (page 130)
- 2 cups (454g) unsalted plant-based butter, room temperature
- 1 tsp pure vanilla extract
- 6 tbsp (90ml) coconut cream
- Pinch of salt

Follow the method for the Vanilla Swiss Meringue Buttercream on page 130, adding the coconut cream, 1 tbsp at a time, and the salt after the vanilla extract. Mix to combine for about 1 minute, using a spatula to scrape down the sides of the bowl as needed.

MOCHA SWISS MERINGUE BUTTERCREAM

MAKES ENOUGH FOR 1 LARGE CAKE OR 24 CUPCAKES

¾ cup (170g) dark plant-based chocolate, chopped

1 recipe Aquafaba Meringue for Swiss Meringue Buttercream (page 129) or 1 recipe Versawhip Meringue for Swiss Meringue Buttercream (page 130)

2 cups (454g) unsalted plant-based butter

Pinch of salt

1 tsp instant espresso granules

Using a double boiler or a glass bowl set atop a small saucepan filled a quarter full of water, heat the chocolate over medium heat until melted. Remove from the heat and set aside to cool.

Follow the method for the Vanilla Swiss Meringue Buttercream on page 130, adding the salt, espresso powder, and melted, cooled chocolate after the butter. Whip for another 15–30 seconds to combine, using a spatula to scrape down the sides of the bowl as needed.

ITALIAN MERINGUE BUTTERCREAMS

For Italian meringue buttercream, you're doing two things in tandem—whipping the meringue and making the sugar syrup. You want to time it so the meringue and syrup are ready around the same time. So go ahead and start your meringue first and let it whip while you set up the sugar to boil.

You need the sugar syrup to reach 240°F (115°C), which is also known as the "soft ball" stage. Use a candy thermometer that rests on the side of the pot to measure this. You needn't stir or disturb the sugar syrup as it bubbles and boils up to its proper temperature.

AQUAFABA MERINGUE FOR ITALIAN BUTTERCREAM
MAKES ABOUT 5 CUPS

2 cans (18 oz/540ml each) unsalted chickpeas

½ tsp cream of tartar

NOTE The reduced aquafaba needs at least 2 hours to chill, and ideally overnight to jell, so start this buttercream preparation ahead of time.

SEPARATE THE AQUAFABA
Pour the chickpeas and their liquid into a strainer set over a medium bowl, straining the aquafaba liquid into the bowl. Reserve the chickpeas for another use.

REDUCE THE AQUAFABA
Transfer the aquafaba liquid to a small saucepan set over medium-high heat. Bring the aquafaba to a low boil (watching that it doesn't boil over), then turn the heat down to low. Simmer the aquafaba until it is reduced by approximately half—you want to end up with roughly 1 cup (250ml) of reduced aquafaba—this could take up to 15 minutes.

CHILL THE AQUAFABA
Once the aquafaba has reduced, remove the saucepan from the heat. Transfer the aquafaba to a heatproof liquid measuring cup or container. Refrigerate, covered, for at least 2 hours and ideally overnight to jell. When reduced aquafaba is refrigerated, it takes on a thick gelatinous consistency. It will be a golden color and it may separate a bit, and all of this is normal.

START WHIPPING THE MERINGUE
In the bowl of a stand mixer fitted with the whisk attachment (make sure both the bowl and whisk attachment are completely grease-free), beat the reduced aquafaba and cream of tartar on high speed until it has thickened into glossy, firm peaks. This may take up to 15 minutes. Leave this meringue in the bowl of the stand mixer, and continue with the method of the buttercream recipe.

BUTTERCREAM DREAMS   135

VERSAWHIP MERINGUE FOR ITALIAN BUTTERCREAM

MAKES ABOUT 5 CUPS

1½ tsp dry Versawhip powder   ¾ cup (185ml) warm water

In a liquid measuring cup, whisk the dry Versawhip powder with the warm water to dissolve.

In the bowl of a stand mixer fitted with the whisk attachment, whisk the Versawhip mixture on low speed for 2 minutes to begin the formation of meringue. Continue whipping until stiff peaks are achieved, 5–8 minutes. Leave this meringue in the bowl of the stand mixer, and continue with the method of the buttercream recipe you're using.

VANILLA ITALIAN MERINGUE BUTTERCREAM

MAKES ENOUGH FOR 1 LARGE CAKE OR 24 CUPCAKES

- 1 recipe Aquafaba Meringue for Italian Buttercream (page 135) or 1 recipe Versawhip Meringue for Italian Buttercream (page 136)
- 2 cups (400g) granulated white sugar
- ⅔ cup (150ml) water
- 2 cups (454g) unsalted plant-based butter, room temperature
- 2 tsp pure vanilla extract
- 2 tsp vanilla bean paste
- Pinch of salt

MAKE THE SYRUP

While the meringue is whipping in the stand mixer, in a medium saucepan set over medium-high heat, stir together the sugar and water. Attach your candy thermometer to the side of the pan. Let the sugar syrup boil undisturbed, getting glassy and bubbly and thicker, until the candy thermometer reads 240°F (115°C), the "soft ball" stage. This may take up to 10 minutes or longer, depending on how hot your stovetop is; gas stovetops tend to heat faster.

ADD THE SYRUP

Once the syrup reaches the desired temperature, keep the meringue whipping and slowly drizzle the hot syrup down the inside of the bowl, being careful not to drizzle on top of the whisk attachment to prevent splattering. Once the syrup has been added, continue to whisk on high speed until the meringue has completely cooled, about 15 minutes.

MAKE THE BUTTERCREAM

With the mixer turned off, swap out the whisk attachment for the paddle attachment.

With the mixer on low speed, add the butter; I use a butter knife and just slice off small pieces of butter right into the mixer. Add the vanilla extract, vanilla bean paste, and salt, whipping for another 15–30 seconds to combine, using a spatula to scrape down the sides of the bowl as needed. Whip on high speed until a glossy, silky frosting forms, about 1 minute. See "Troubleshooting Meringue Buttercream" on page 122.

Store any leftover buttercream in an airtight container in the fridge for up to 1 week.

> **NOTE:** When pouring the hot syrup into the meringue, make sure you pour slowly down the side of the bowl, avoiding the moving whisk itself to prevent splatters. Whip for another 15 minutes or so after the hot syrup has been added, to ensure your meringue has completely cooled down before adding the room-temperature butter.

136 PLANTCAKES

RASPBERRY ITALIAN MERINGUE BUTTERCREAM

MAKES ENOUGH FOR 1 LARGE CAKE OR 24 CUPCAKES

- 1 recipe Aquafaba Meringue for Italian Buttercream (page 135) or 1 recipe Versawhip Meringue for Italian Buttercream (page 136)
- 2 cups (400g) granulated white sugar
- ⅔ cup (150ml) water
- 2 cups (454g) unsalted plant-based butter, room temperature
- ¼ cup (30g) freeze-dried raspberries, powdered
- 2 tsp pure vanilla extract
- Pinch of salt

Follow the method for the Vanilla Italian Meringue Buttercream on page 136, adding the powdered freeze-dried raspberries, vanilla extract, and salt after the butter.

LEMON ITALIAN MERINGUE BUTTERCREAM

MAKES ENOUGH FOR 1 LARGE CAKE OR 24 CUPCAKES

- 1 recipe Aquafaba Meringue for Italian Buttercream (page 135) or 1 recipe Versawhip Meringue for Italian Buttercream (page 136)
- 2 cups (400g) granulated white sugar
- ⅔ cup (150ml) water
- 2 cups (454g) unsalted plant-based butter, room temperature
- 1 tbsp fresh lemon juice
- 2 tsp pure vanilla extract
- Pinch of salt

Follow the method for the Vanilla Italian Meringue Buttercream on page 136, adding the lemon juice, vanilla extract, and salt after the butter.

MAPLE ITALIAN MERINGUE BUTTERCREAM

MAKES ENOUGH FOR 1 LARGE CAKE OR 24 CUPCAKES

- 1 recipe Aquafaba Meringue for Italian Buttercream (page 135) or 1 recipe Versawhip Meringue for Italian Buttercream (page 136)
- 1½ cups (375ml) pure maple syrup
- 2 cups (454g) unsalted plant-based butter, room temperature
- Pinch of salt

> This is very similar to an Italian meringue style buttercream, but uses maple syrup instead of hot sugar syrup.

Follow the method for the Vanilla Italian Meringue Buttercream on page 136, but instead of using the sugar and water to make a syrup, heat the maple syrup to 240°F (115°C), the "soft ball" stage. Add the salt after the butter.

BUTTERCREAM DREAMS 137

OTHER FROSTINGS + ONE VERY BERRY QUICK JAM

CHOCOLATE GANACHE FROSTING

MAKES ENOUGH FOR 1 LARGE CAKE OR 24 CUPCAKES

- 2 cups (500ml) full-fat coconut milk or plant milk
- 2½ cups (450g) callets or finely chopped pieces bittersweet or dark plant-based chocolate

In a medium saucepan set over medium-high heat, bring the milk to a very low boil, keeping an eye on it to ensure it doesn't burn or bubble over.

Remove the pan from the heat and gently add the chocolate to the pan so the hot milk covers the chocolate completely. Let the mixture stand untouched for 10 minutes. Then slowly whisk the mixture until a shiny, smooth ganache forms.

Let cool in the fridge or freezer until it's a thick, spreadable consistency—in the fridge this will take at least an hour, or you can power-cool it in the freezer for 25–30 minutes (but keep an eye on it to make sure it doesn't freeze).

Once it has cooled and thickened, transfer the ganache to the bowl of a stand mixer fitted with the paddle attachment. Beat on high speed until it has whipped into a delectable frosting. Make sure the ganache has cooled completely before whipping, otherwise your frosting may be too loose. If you find it too loose, add a little icing sugar, 1 tbsp at a time, to help thicken it.

Store any leftover ganache in an airtight container in the fridge for up to 3 days.

FUDGY CARAMEL FROSTING

MAKES ENOUGH FOR 1 SINGLE-LAYER CAKE

- ¼ cup (56g) unsalted plant-based butter
- ½ cup (100g) light brown sugar
- ¼ cup (60ml) soy creamer
- 1 tbsp water
- ¼ cup (32g) icing sugar, sifted
- Pinch of fine sea salt

In a saucepan set over medium heat, heat the butter, brown sugar, soy creamer, and water. Bring the mixture to a full rolling boil and cook for 3 minutes. Turn off the heat and let the mixture cool for an additional 3 minutes, stirring once or twice to help cool it down.

After 3 minutes, whisk in the icing sugar and salt until the mixture is smooth and slightly thickened. Use immediately to frost your cooled cake before the frosting develops a crust.

BUTTERCREAM DREAMS

TANGY YOGURT FROSTING

MAKES ENOUGH FOR 1 SINGLE-LAYER CAKE

- ½ cup (112g) unsalted plant-based butter, room temperature
- 1 cup (250ml) best-quality plain plant-based yogurt
- 2 cups (260g) icing sugar, sifted
- 1 tbsp potato starch or cornstarch
- 1 tsp pure vanilla extract
- 1 tsp lemon zest
- Pinch of salt + more to taste

In the bowl of a stand mixer fitted with the paddle attachment, beat the butter on high speed until fluffy, using a spatula to scrape down the sides of the bowl as needed. Add the yogurt and mix on low speed for 30 seconds to incorporate. Add the icing sugar and potato starch or cornstarch and pulse on low speed to combine. Add the vanilla extract, lemon zest, and salt. Beat the mixture on medium speed to combine, about 30 seconds.

MAPLE CREAM CHEESE FROSTING

MAKES ENOUGH FOR 1 SINGLE-LAYER CAKE

- ½ cup (112g) plant-based cream cheese, room temperature
- ½ cup (112g) unsalted plant-based butter, room temperature
- 1 cup (130g) icing sugar, sifted
- 3 tbsp pure maple syrup
- Pinch of salt + more to taste

In the bowl of a stand mixer fitted with the paddle attachment, beat the cream cheese, butter, icing sugar, maple syrup, and salt on medium speed until combined, about 1 minute. The frosting will be a little loose but thick enough to dollop onto the cake and gently spread to the edges.

> **NOTE:** You can try thickening the frosting by adding more icing sugar; however, this will add extra sweetness, so proceed with caution!

YOU GOT JAMMED (A VERY BERRY QUICK JAM RECIPE)

MAKES ABOUT 2 CUPS (500ML)

Quick jam can be slathered on pancakes, dolloped on waffles, or, for the purposes of this book, spread between cake layers. Nestling jam against creamy frosting and soft cake creates the perfect tangy sweet blast of dreamy fruit. For this recipe, you can use raspberries, strawberries, blueberries, or any fruit, really. (One time I made ONE single jar of Concord grape jam for my grape-jam-loving mother-in-law. I had bought a brown paper bag of plump, candy-sweet Concord grapes at the farmers' market and knew what I had to do, haha.) The delight of quick jam is that you can bump up the sugar or reduce the sugar to your liking, because it will be used imminently. Thank you to Camilla Wynne for further teaching me about the beauty and ease of jam making. For a great resource on deep jamming, canning, and using preserves in baking, I suggest picking up Camilla's book *Jam Bake*!

This recipe makes enough to use as a cake filling and have leftovers to spread on pancakes as a little treat!

2½ cups (375g) fresh or frozen berries, cleaned + hulled and sliced if we're talking strawberries

2 cups (400g) granulated white sugar

2 tbsp fresh lemon juice

Pinch of salt

In a large bowl, combine the berries, sugar, lemon juice, and salt and let sit for 15 minutes or so to macerate and get all juicy.

In a medium saucepan set over medium-high heat, cook the berry mixture, stirring frequently. It will bubble up to a decent boil; keep cooking and stirring gently—being careful not to burn the berries, and reducing the heat a little if needed—until it has thickened into a jam-like consistency, about 30 minutes. (Be careful not to overcook it, as that can create a "cranberry jelly" situation where the jam is *too* thick—still delicious, but harder to spread.)

Remove the jam from the heat and let cool completely before using. Store in a tightly sealed glass jar in the fridge for up to 1 week, if you haven't gobbled it up by then.

BUTTERCREAM DREAMS

5

FANCIFUL WILDCARD CAKES

Giant Chocolate Chip Cookie Cake

2⅛ cups (300g) all-purpose flour

½ tsp baking soda

½ tsp baking powder

1 tsp fine sea salt

1 cup (224g) unsalted plant-based butter, room temperature

¾ cup + 2 tbsp (175g) brown sugar

½ cup (100g) granulated white sugar

¼ cup (50g) turbinado sugar

2 tsp pure vanilla extract

¼ cup (60ml) water

2 cups (350g) callets or chopped pieces best-quality dark or semisweet plant-based chocolate

Flaky sea salt

Frosting

½ recipe Vanilla Buttercream (page 125)

Pink and turquoise gel colors (or the colors of your choice)

Rainbow sprinkles

Edible flowers (optional)

GIANT CHOCOLATE CHIP COOKIE CAKE WITH VANILLA BUTTERCREAM

MAKES ONE 10-INCH COOKIE CAKE

One of my favorite things in the world is a freshly baked chocolate chip cookie, cooled slightly on the pan, tiny flakes of sea salt nestled into the shiny, melty chocolate . . . I am so excited to include a chocolate chip cookie recipe in this book—technically it's more of a chocolate "chunk" recipe, as it uses dairy-free chocolate in either chopped or callet form (although of course a high-quality chocolate chip will work wonderfully too!). This recipe is adapted from a recipe by my baking buddy Erin Clarkson of Cloudy Kitchen—she is the cookie MASTER, and I was so excited to veganize my favorite recipe of hers. I know using three types of sugar seems outrageous, but the turbinado sugar (also known as raw sugar) gives it the most delightful sandy texture. If you don't have turbinado sugar, you can replace it with additional granulated white sugar.

NOTE: You can make this cookie in a variety of larger round cake pan sizes, just keep in mind that the baking time will differ.

MAKE THE COOKIE CAKE

Preheat the oven to 350°F (175°C). Prepare a 10- × 2-inch round cake pan by spritzing it with vegetable oil or generously buttering the entire pan, and lining with a parchment paper circle cut to size, and then spritzing again with oil, to prevent sticking.

In a medium bowl, whisk together the all-purpose flour, baking soda, baking powder, and salt.

In the bowl of a stand mixer fitted with the paddle attachment, beat the butter, brown sugar, white sugar, and turbinado sugar on high speed until light and fluffy, about 2 minutes. Scrape down the sides of the bowl and add the vanilla extract and water, beating to combine.

With the mixer turned off, add the flour mixture, then pulse to just combine. Mix on low speed for 15–20 seconds to fully combine. Add the chopped chocolate or chocolate pieces, and pulse to combine.

continued

FANCIFUL WILDCARD CAKES

BAKE THE CAKE

Transfer the dough to the prepared cake pan. Using a spatula, flatten the dough to fit the shape of the pan in an even layer without pressing down too firmly.

Bake for 22–26 minutes, until the top and edges of the cake are lightly browned. Sprinkle with flaky sea salt and let the cake cool completely in the pan set on top of a wire rack.

ASSEMBLE THE CAKE

Remove the cooled cake from the pan and place on a cake board or platter. Dollop a generous amount of the vanilla frosting onto the center of the cake. Using an offset spatula, spread a thick layer of the frosting towards the edges of the cake.

Divide the remaining buttercream between two small bowls and use just a touch of gel color to tint each bowl of buttercream a different color. Fit two piping bags with the open star tips of your choosing. Pipe a border around the cake, alternating the butterceam colors as you go (see page 27).

If you would like to add a buttercream message to the cake, fill a piping bag pitted with a small open circle tip with some of the remaining buttercream and pipe out your message.

Sprinkle generously with your favorite rainbow sprinkles and a few edible flowers, if desired.

This cake will taste freshest eaten within a day of making it, but can be stored in the fridge, covered, for up to 3 days. See page 13 for storage notes.

Vanilla Cake

1¼ cups (310ml) soy milk

2 tsp apple cider vinegar

½ cup (125ml) aquafaba (see page 8)

½ cup (112g) unsalted plant-based butter

½ cup (125ml) vegetable oil

1½ cups (300g) granulated white sugar

1 tbsp pure vanilla extract

1 tsp vanilla bean paste

3 cups (390g) cake flour

1 tbsp baking powder

1 tsp baking soda

¾ tsp fine sea salt

Coffee Syrup Soak

¼ cup + 2 tbsp (90ml) strong, hot coffee

¼ cup (50g) granulated white sugar

1 tsp pure vanilla extract

Filling + Frosting

Blueberry jam (page 141) or use your favorite store-bought

1 recipe Maple Italian Meringue Buttercream (page 137)

Fresh blueberries

Edible flowers (I use bachelor's button petals)

FANCY BREAKFAST CAKE WITH MAPLE ITALIAN MERINGUE BUTTERCREAM, COFFEE SYRUP + BLUEBERRY JAM

MAKES ONE 7-INCH 3-LAYER CAKE

The title's a mouthful but so is the cake—a mouthful of DELICIOUSNESS! Our neighbor's daughter described it as tasting like a "fancy breakfast," which sounded like the perfect name for it, so it stuck. Inspired entirely by the wonderful Camilla Wynne of the Preservation Society, this is the plant-based version of her maple Italian meringue buttercream-frosted vanilla cake with coffee syrup–soaked layers and blueberry jam. (I made this one for my beloved Auntie Cor's ninetieth birthday!)

MAKE THE CAKE

Preheat the oven to 350°F (175°C). Prepare three 7- × 2-inch round cake pans by spritzing them with vegetable oil and lining with parchment circles cut to size, and then spritzing again with oil, to prevent sticking.

In a small bowl, mix the soy milk with the apple cider vinegar and set aside for 10 minutes to thicken. It may look a bit separated at this point, but that's normal.

In a small bowl, whisk the aquafaba until foamy and light, about 1 minute, and set aside.

In the bowl of a stand mixer fitted with the paddle attachment, cream together the butter, vegetable oil, and sugar until creamy and blended well. Add the aquafaba, vanilla extract, and vanilla bean paste, mixing until combined.

In a large bowl, whisk together the cake flour, baking powder, baking soda, and salt.

With the mixer on low speed, alternate between adding the flour mixture and the milk and vinegar mixture, beginning and ending with the flour mixture, until just combined. Use a spatula to fold in any stray flour lumps, but try not to overmix the batter.

continued

BAKE THE CAKE

Divide the cake batter evenly between the prepared pans. Give the pans a light tap on the counter to reduce any air bubbles. Bake for 22–25 minutes, until the cake edges are lightly browned, and a toothpick inserted into the center comes out with only moist crumbs.

Let the cakes cool completely in their pans set on top of wire racks.

MAKE THE COFFEE SYRUP

In a small bowl, whisk together the hot coffee, sugar, and vanilla extract. Let cool completely before using.

ASSEMBLE THE CAKE

Follow the steps on pages 19–22 to fill and frost the cake using the blueberry jam and maple Italian meringue buttercream, to the final frost stage. While building the cake layers, add the coffee syrup to each layer, and follow the jam dam or dugout pool method to carve out a small pool in the center of the buttercream and add blueberry jam to the layers. For the photo on page 148, I used a smooth style for my second layer of frosting.

Fit a piping bag with a leaf tip and fill the bag with 1 cup (250ml) of the buttercream. Pipe buttercream swags onto the cake (see page 28), repeating until the cake is all swagged out! Fill a piping bag fitted with an open star tip and fill with any remaining buttercream, to create ruffly shell borders (see page 28) on the top and bottom edges of the cake.

Top with fresh blueberries and edible flowers.

This cake will taste freshest eaten within a day of making it, but can be stored in the fridge, covered, for up to 3 days. See page 13 for storage notes.

Earl Grey Tea Cake

- ½ cup (112g) unsalted plant-based butter
- ¼ cup (16g) Earl Grey tea leaves (about 4 tea bags, cut open to use the leaves)
- 1¼ cups (310ml) soy milk
- 2 tsp apple cider vinegar
- ½ cup (125ml) aquafaba (see page 8)
- 3 cups (390g) cake flour
- 1 tbsp baking powder
- 1 tsp baking soda
- 1 tsp fine sea salt
- ½ cup (125ml) vegetable oil
- 1½ cups (300g) granulated white sugar
- 2 tsp pure vanilla extract

Earl Grey Tea Syrup

- 1 cup (200g) granulated white sugar
- 1 cup (250ml) water
- 4 Earl Grey tea bags

Toffee Bits

- 1 cup (224g) unsalted plant-based butter
- 1¼ cups (250g) granulated white sugar
- 1 tbsp pure maple syrup
- ½ cup (125ml) soy milk
- 1 tsp fine sea salt

Filling + Frosting

- 1 recipe Lemon Italian Meringue Buttercream (page 137)
- ¼ cup (15g) freeze-dried raspberries, powdered
- 3 gel colors of your choice

DANCE LIKE NO ONE IS WATCHING EARL GREY CAKE WITH LEMON ITALIAN MERINGUE BUTTERCREAM

MAKES ONE 7-INCH 3-LAYER CAKE

There is this gorgeous trend of maximalist cake designs going around that looks so liberating, fun, and fancy free—piped buttercream ruffles in a myriad of colors, wildly delicious-sounding flavors and fillings . . . Admittedly I have always been sort of rigid and exacting in my cake designing, and seeing these cakes made me want to LIBERATE MY MIND and "cake like no one is watching." It's like how when my son, Teddy, in his younger child years, would decorate a birthday cake for my husband, Rich, in a whimsical mish-mash. This truly delicious, maximalist cake has Earl Grey tea cake layers, Lemon Italian Meringue Buttercream (page 137), and homemade toffee bits, and is piped in the Lambeth vintage style.

MAKE THE CAKE

Preheat the oven to 350°F (175°C). Prepare three 7- × 2-inch round cake pans by spritzing them with vegetable oil and lining with parchment paper circles cut to size, and then spritzing again with oil, to prevent sticking.

In a small saucepan, melt the butter over low heat. Add the loose tea leaves, remove from heat, and let stand for 10 minutes. Strain the butter to remove the tea leaves and let the tea butter cool for 5 minutes.

In a small bowl, mix the soy milk with the apple cider vinegar and set aside for 10 minutes to thicken. It may look a bit separated at this point, but that's normal.

Whisk the aquafaba until foamy and light, about 1 minute, and set aside.

In a medium bowl, whisk together the cake flour, baking powder, baking soda, and salt to combine.

continued

In the bowl of a stand mixer fitted with the paddle attachment, mix the tea butter with the vegetable oil and sugar until creamy and well blended. Add the foamy aquafaba and vanilla extract, mixing until combined.

With the mixer on low speed, alternate between adding the flour mixture and soy milk mixture, beginning and ending with the flour mixture, mixing until combined and a smooth batter forms, about 30 seconds total. To avoid overmixing, if needed, finish the batter by hand using a rubber spatula for a few more turns until completely incorporated.

BAKE THE CAKE

Divide the batter evenly between the prepared pans, evening out the batter with an offset spatula if needed. Give the pans a light tap on the counter to reduce any air bubbles.

Bake for 22–25 minutes, or until the cakes are lightly golden around the edges, and a toothpick inserted in the center comes out with only moist crumbs.

Let the cakes cool completely in their pans set on top of wire racks.

MAKE THE EARL GREY TEA SYRUP

In a small saucepan set over medium-high heat, heat the sugar and water until the sugar has dissolved completely. Let the syrup bubble for a minute or so before removing from the heat. Add the tea bags, allowing them to steep for 10 minutes. Squish out any "tea liquid" remaining in the tea bags into the syrup, and discard the tea bags. Whisk gently, then let the syrup cool completely before using.

MAKE THE TOFFEE BITS

Line a baking sheet with parchment paper. Attach a candy thermometer to the side of a heavy-bottomed saucepan set over medium-high heat and add the butter, sugar, maple syrup, soy milk, and salt, stirring constantly and melting everything together, until the mixture begins to boil, being careful nothing boils over!

Continue stirring (you may get a bit sweaty) until the mixture is bubbling and turning an amber color. Keep stirring until the mixture reaches "soft crack" stage on the candy thermometer—approximately 275°F–290°F (135°C–143°C). Immediately pour the candy mixture onto the prepared baking sheet, spreading it with an offset spatula to the edges of the parchment paper. Let cool completely before breaking up into pieces (use a rolling pin to crush the small toffee bits). Store the toffee in an airtight container for up to 1 week.

ASSEMBLE THE CAKE

Follow the steps on pages 19–22 to fill and frost the cake using the lemon Italian meringue buttercream, to the final frost stage. Before adding frosting to each layer, soak the cake layer with the Earl Grey Tea Syrup. For the photo opposite, I used a smooth style for the second layer of frosting.

To decorate the cake, first create a raspberry lemon buttercream: scoop 1 cup (250ml) of the remaining lemon buttercream into a small bowl and, using a spatula, carefully fold in the powdered freeze-dried raspberries. Fit a piping bag with an open star tip and fill the bag with the raspberry lemon buttercream.

Divide the remaining lemon buttercream between three small bowls and use just a touch of gel color to tint each bowl of buttercream (I used yellow, turquoise, and cornflower blue). Fit three additional piping bags with different tips: I used a large leaf tip for the yellow ruffles and an open star tip for the blue and turquoise. Pipe and decorate the cake to your heart's content, adding piped borders and plenty of ruffly swags (see page 28).

This cake will taste freshest eaten within a day of making it, but can be stored in the fridge, covered, for up to 3 days. See page 13 for storage notes.

Meringue Mushrooms (see note)

1 recipe Aquafaba Meringue for Swiss Meringue Buttercream (page 129)

¼ tsp red gel color or 1 tsp supercolor powder

Chocolate Cake

1 cup (250ml) soy milk

1 tsp apple cider vinegar

2 cups (280g) all-purpose flour

2 cups (400g) granulated white sugar

¾ cup (90g) Dutch-process cocoa powder

1 tsp baking powder

1 tsp baking soda

1 tsp fine sea salt

½ cup (125ml) vegetable oil

2 tsp pure vanilla extract

1 cup (250ml) strong, hot coffee

Chocolate Bark

1½ cups (200g) chopped best-quality bittersweet or dark plant-based chocolate

Pistachio Cookie Moss

1 cup (140g) all-purpose flour

½ tsp baking powder

½ tsp fine sea salt

¼ cup (112g) unsalted plant-based butter, room temperature

½ cup (100g) granulated white sugar

1 tsp pure vanilla extract

1 tsp pistachio extract or almond extract (optional)

¼ tsp moss-green gel color or 2 tsp supercolor powder

Filling + Frosting

1 recipe Chocolate Buttercream (page 125)

HOLIDAY VIBES CHOCOLATE STUMP CAKE

MAKES ONE 7-INCH 3-LAYER CAKE

I have always loved the delightfully 1980s Yule Log–style cake, traditionally made as a roll cake. This chocolate stump cake is in the same woodland holiday family as the yule log, covered with chocolate bark shards and festooned with red-capped meringue mushrooms and green pistachio cookie moss. Although it has quite a few components, I promise that it will be a very hilarious and fun centerpiece at your holiday gathering or woodland-themed party. You can break down the steps and make the components over a few days. For instance, the cake layers can be baked, cooled, and then frozen until needed; the meringue mushrooms and cookie moss can be made a day ahead too. This could be a fun group project to make with kids, or a gaggle of friends—get those holiday tunes cranking, roll up your sleeves, and jump in!

 Ideally, you will leave the meringue kisses to dry overnight, so plan ahead for this recipe.

MAKE THE MERINGUE MUSHROOMS

Divide the meringue between two bowls. Carefully fold in the gel color to one bowl of the meringue, being careful to not deflate the meringue.

Preheat the oven to 200°F (95°C). Line a baking sheet with parchment paper. Add a tiny amount of meringue to the bottom of the parchment paper to stick it to the baking sheet.

Fit each of two piping bags with an open circle tip and fill with meringue—one with the white meringue for the mushroom stems, and one with the red meringue for the mushroom caps.

Pipe white mushroom stems by squeezing the piping bag and pulling upward. Try a variety of thicknesses and heights, if desired.

continued

FANCIFUL WILDCARD CAKES

Pipe red mushroom caps by piping a meringue-kiss-like shape, then use a lightly-dampened finger to press gently down on it to remove any "point" shape.

Bake for 1½ hours, making sure they aren't browning, until dried out and not sticky to the touch. Turn the oven off, and let them dry out completely overnight in the oven, if you can.

Once the stems and caps are completely dry, stick them together with a tiny piped amount of the chocolate buttercream. Store leftover caps and piped stems in an airtight container in a cool, dry place for up to 1 week.

MAKE THE CAKE

Preheat the oven to 350°F (175°C). Prepare three 7- × 2-inch round cake pans by spritzing them with vegetable oil and lining with parchment paper circles cut to size. Spray again to prevent sticking.

In a small bowl, mix the soy milk with the apple cider vinegar and set aside for 10 minutes to thicken. It may look a bit separated at this point, but that's normal.

In the bowl of a stand mixer fitted with the paddle attachment, combine the flour, sugar, cocoa powder, baking powder, baking soda, and salt on low speed.

In a medium bowl, whisk together the soy milk mixture, vegetable oil, and vanilla extract.

With the mixer still on low speed, add the oil mixture. Pour in the hot coffee and mix until combined and a smooth batter forms, 15–30 seconds, using a spatula to scrape down the sides of the bowl as needed.

BAKE THE CAKE

Divide the batter evenly between the prepared cake pans. Tap each pan gently on the counter to reduce any air bubbles. Bake for 22–25 minutes, or until the cake is lightly domed, has pulled away from the sides slightly, and a toothpick inserted into the center of the cake comes out with only moist crumbs.

Let the cakes cool completely in their pans set on top of wire racks.

MAKE THE CHOCOLATE BARK

Line a small baking sheet (it needs to be able to fit in your fridge) with parchment paper.

In a small saucepan or double boiler, carefully melt the chocolate over low heat, making sure it does not burn. Once melted, pour the chocolate onto the prepared baking sheet, using an offset spatula to spread it in a thin, even layer to the edges of the parchment paper. Chill in the fridge for about 30 minutes to set.

Using clean hands (or wearing food-safe gloves), carefully break the chocolate into shards of varying sizes, not handling it too much to avoid marking up the bark or melting the bark with warm, over-excited fingers. Any leftover bark can be stored in an airtight container in a cool, dry place for up to 1 week—chop it up to sprinkle over sundaes or just eat as is.

MAKE THE PISTACHIO COOKIE MOSS

Preheat the oven to 350°F (175°C). Line a baking sheet with parchment paper and set aside.

In a small bowl, whisk together the flour, baking powder, and salt.

In the bowl of a stand mixer fitted with the paddle attachment, beat together the butter and sugar until fluffy, scraping down the sides of the bowl as needed. Add the vanilla extract and pistachio or almond extract, and mix on medium speed for 15 seconds to incorporate. Add the dry ingredients and mix on low speed to incorporate into a dough, 15–20 seconds. Add the gel color or supercolor powder and mix until incorporated, 15–20 seconds.

Using an offset spatula, spread out a small clump of the cookie dough into a thin abstract shape. Continue making thin shapes of dough, filling the cookie sheet. Bake for 8–10 minutes.

Let the cookies cool completely before breaking them up into moss chunks and crumbs. Any leftover cookie pieces can be stored in an airtight container in a cool, dry place for up to 1 week.

ASSEMBLE THE CAKE

STUMP TIME! Follow the steps on pages 19–22 to fill and frost the cake to the final frost stage, using the chocolate buttercream. For the photo opposite, I used an au naturel style for the second layer of frosting.

DECORATE THE CAKE

After applying the second buttercream coat, carefully place the shards of chocolate bark vertically on the sides of the cake, gently pressing them in with parchment paper to stick them to the buttercream. (I use parchment paper to do this to shield the bark from my warm fingers!) Work your way around the cake, placing pieces of bark in varying sizes to cover the buttercream.

Sprinkle the pistachio cookie moss pieces in varying sizes on top of the cake. Place some meringue mushrooms on the top of the cake and along the bottom edge of the cake, if desired.

This cake will taste freshest enjoyed within a day of making it, but can be stored in the fridge, covered, for up to 3 days. See page 13 for more storage notes.

FANCIFUL WILDCARD CAKES   157

Black Sesame Cake

½ cup (70g) toasted black sesame seeds

¼ cup (60ml) light corn syrup

¼ cup (60ml) pure maple syrup

2 cups (260g) cake flour

¾ cup (105g) finely ground toasted black sesame seeds

2 tsp baking powder

¾ tsp fine sea salt

½ tsp baking soda

¾ cup (170g) unsalted plant-based butter, room temperature

1¼ cups (250g) granulated white sugar

1 tsp pure vanilla extract

1 cup (250ml) full-fat coconut milk

Vanilla Simple Syrup

1 cup (200g) granulated white sugar

1 cup (250ml) water

1 tsp pure vanilla extract

Black Sesame Brittle

1½ cups (300g) granulated white sugar

2 tbsp water

¾ cup (105g) toasted black sesame seeds

Pinch of sea salt

Flaky sea salt to finish

Filling + Frosting

1 recipe Coconut Swiss Meringue Buttercream (page 132)

BLACK SESAME BRITTLE CAKE WITH COCONUT SWISS MERINGUE BUTTERCREAM

MAKES ONE 7-INCH 3-LAYER CAKE

The angular black sesame brittle fragments on this cake remind me of my old bandmate's brooch collection—black sparkly brooches were part of his signature look back when we played in a post-punk synth (goth) band together many years ago. The brittle is also very addictive, reminiscent of the sticky-sweet but satisfyingly crisp Sesame Snaps we ate as kids. Crush a portion of the brittle up into textural crumbs of varying sizes to press into the buttercream layers for even more crunch! Look for toasted black sesame seeds at your local Asian supermarkets, or online with the usual suspects.

MAKE THE CAKE

Preheat the oven to 350°F (175°C). Prepare three 7- × 2-inch round cake pans by spritzing them with vegetable oil and lining with parchment circles cut to size, and then spritzing again with oil, to prevent sticking.

In a food processor, combine the toasted sesame seeds, corn syrup, and maple syrup and blend into a paste.

In a medium bowl, whisk together the cake flour, ground black sesame seeds, baking powder, salt, and baking soda.

In the bowl of a stand mixer fitted with the paddle attachment, beat the butter, sugar, sesame paste, and vanilla extract on high speed to combine, scraping down the sides of the bowl as needed.

With the mixer on low speed, alternate between adding the flour mixture and the coconut milk, beginning and ending with the dry ingredients. Mix on low speed until a batter forms, 15–30 seconds.

continued

BAKE THE CAKE

Divide the batter evenly between the prepared cake pans. Give the pans a light tap on the counter to reduce any air bubbles. Bake for 22–24 minutes, until a toothpick inserted into the center of the cake comes out with only moist crumbs.

Let the cakes cool completely in their pans set on top of wire racks.

MAKE THE VANILLA SIMPLE SYRUP

In a small saucepan set over medium-high heat, heat the sugar and water, allowing the sugar to dissolve and the mixture to reduce, 5–10 minutes. Remove from the heat and stir in the vanilla extract. Let cool completely before using. The syrup can be stored in the fridge for up to 2 weeks.

MAKE THE BLACK SESAME BRITTLE

Line a large baking sheet with parchment paper. In a medium saucepan set over medium-high heat, combine the sugar and water. Heat the mixture until it turns a dark amber color and registers 300°F (150°C) on a candy thermometer, 8–10 minutes, depending on your stovetop.

Remove the mixture from the heat and carefully stir in the sesame seeds and salt. Working quickly, pour the mixture onto the prepared baking sheet, spreading in an even layer. Allow to harden and cool for about 5 minutes, then add an even, light sprinkle of flaky sea salt. Let cool completely, about 30 minutes, before breaking into fragments and brittle crumbs.

ASSEMBLE THE CAKE

Follow the steps on pages 19–22 to fill and frost the cake to the final frost stage using the coconut Swiss meringue buttercream. Add the vanilla simple syrup to the cake layers as you build the cake. Crush up some of the brittle into little pieces and then sprinkle it on the coconut buttercream layers, pressing it into the buttercream. For the second layer of frosting in the photo on page 158, I used the au naturel style of frosting.

Press black sesame brittle fragments onto the sides and top of the cake.

This cake will taste freshest eaten within a day of making it, but can be stored in the fridge, covered, for up to 3 days. See page 13 for storage notes.

Matcha Cake

1 cup (250ml) soy milk

1 cup (300g) plant-based sour cream

5 tbsp (75ml) aquafaba (see page 8)

1 tsp pure vanilla extract

¼ tsp moss-green gel color (optional)

2½ cups (325g) cake flour

1½ cups (300g) granulated white sugar

2 tbsp matcha powder

2 tsp baking powder

¾ tsp fine sea salt

⅔ cup (150g) unsalted plant-based butter

Matcha Syrup

½ cup (125ml) water

½ cup (100g) granulated white sugar

1 tsp matcha powder

Matcha Cookie/Mini Cookies/Crumble

½ cup (100g) granulated white sugar

1 tbsp golden brown sugar

¾ cup (96g) cake flour

1 tsp matcha powder

½ tsp baking powder

½ tsp fine sea salt

¼ cup (60ml) vegetable oil

Tiny amount of moss-green gel color (optional)

Filling + Frosting

1 recipe Raspberry Swiss Meringue Buttercream (page 131)

Fresh raspberries

MATCHA GREEN TEA CAKE WITH RASPBERRY SWISS MERINGUE BUTTERCREAM + MATCHA MINI COOKIES

MAKES ONE 7-INCH 3-LAYER CAKE

Earthy green tea meets floral raspberry notes in this layer cake worthy of a dainty tea party. I love the look of the light-pink raspberry Swiss meringue buttercream—which is made tangy and deeply raspberry flavored thanks to our special friend, freeze-dried raspberries. Matcha green tea powder can be found at specialty tea shops and Asian grocery stores or online. For the matcha cookie topping, you're essentially making a big old sweet and salty earthy matcha-flavored sugar cookie that you break up into cookie crumble bits for yummy texture and to sprinkle on top, or you can cut out matcha mini cookies instead, which add a cute design element.

MAKE THE CAKE

Preheat the oven to 325°F (165°C). Prepare three 7- × 2-inch round cake pans by spritzing them with vegetable oil and lining with parchment circles cut to size, and then spritzing again with oil, to prevent sticking.

In a large bowl using a balloon whisk, whisk the soy milk, sour cream, aquafaba, vanilla extract, and green gel color vigorously together until combined and frothy.

In the bowl of a stand mixer fitted with the paddle attachment, mix together the flour, sugar, matcha powder, baking powder, and salt until combined.

continued

With the mixer on low speed, add the butter, 1-inch pieces at a time (I just use a butter knife to slice off pieces from the brick of butter right into the bowl). The mixture should clump up and look as if there are some coarse sand–like pieces in there.

With the mixer still on low, pour in half of the whipped milk mixture, mixing for about 15 seconds to incorporate. Pour in the remaining milk mixture and mix until a smooth batter forms, about 30 seconds. To avoid overmixing, if needed, finish the batter by hand using a rubber spatula for a few more turns until completely incorporated.

BAKE THE CAKE

Divide the batter evenly between the prepared cake pans, evening out the batter with an offset spatula if needed. Give the pans a light tap on the counter to reduce any air bubbles. Bake for 22–25 minutes, until the cakes are lightly golden around the edges, and a toothpick inserted in the center comes out with only moist crumbs.

Let the cakes cool completely in their pans set on top of wire racks.

MAKE THE MATCHA SYRUP

In a small saucepan set over medium heat, whisk the water, sugar, and matcha powder until the mixture is fully incorporated, there are no matcha lumps, and the sugar has completely dissolved. Allow it to reduce for a few minutes on the stovetop. Remove from the heat and let cool completely before using. The syrup will thicken somewhat as it cools, and you can power-chill it in the fridge or freezer to speed up the process.

MAKE THE MATCHA COOKIE

Preheat the oven to 300°F (150°C). Line a baking sheet with parchment paper.

In a medium bowl, combine the white sugar, brown sugar, flour, matcha powder, baking powder, and salt, mixing until combined. Add the vegetable oil and a tiny amount of gel color. Use a spatula to mix to combine.

Turn the dough out onto the prepared baking sheet, flattening and separating it into smaller pieces with an offset spatula. Alternatively, use a large piping tip to cut out mini circle cookies, if desired (as pictured opposite).

Bake for 15 minutes, until lightly golden. Let the cookies cool and crisp up completely before breaking up into cookie crumble pieces, if making a crumble.

ASSEMBLE THE CAKE

Follow the steps on pages 19–22 to fill and frost the cake, to the final frost stage, adding the matcha syrup to each layer, and using the raspberry Swiss meringue buttercream as the filling. For the photo opposite, I made mine a naked cake by scraping all around the sides to reveal the inner buttercream layers (see page 22).

Fit a piping bag with a large multi-pronged open star tip and fill the bag with the remaining raspberry Swiss meringue buttercream. Add piped drop stars, fresh raspberries, and the mini matcha cookies or matcha crumble to the top of the cake.

This cake will taste freshest eaten within a day of making it, but can be stored in the fridge, covered, for up to 3 days. See page 13 for storage notes.

Chocolate Hazelnut Meringue Layers

1½ cups (168g) finely ground skinless toasted hazelnuts

½ cup (65g) icing sugar, sifted

¼ cup (30g) Dutch-process cocoa powder

1 recipe Aquafaba Meringue for Swiss Meringue Buttercream (page 129) or 1 recipe Versawhip Meringue for Swiss Meringue Buttercream (page 130)

Filling + Frosting

1 recipe Chocolate Ganache Frosting (page 139)

1 recipe Mocha Swiss Meringue Buttercream (page 133)

Fresh raspberries

Edible flower petals (optional)

MOCHA DACQUOISE CAKE

MAKES ONE 8-INCH 3-LAYER CAKE

Ya nut cake, you! By now it's quite obvious that I love me some crunch and texture in my desserts, and this mocha dacquoise delivers on all factors with crispy, chewy chocolate meringue layers made from ground toasted hazelnuts—told you this was a nut cake!—layered with rich, creamy chocolate ganache, fresh raspberries, and mocha Swiss meringue buttercream, then decorated with piped buttercream and more fresh berries to finish. You can dust it lightly with cocoa powder and add edible flower petals too, if desired.

MAKE THE MERINGUE LAYERS

Preheat the oven to 250°F (120°C). Line two baking sheets with parchment paper. Using an 8- × 2-inch round cake pan as your outline, draw two circles in pencil on the first sheet, and one circle on the second. Flip the papers over.

In a medium bowl, make the dacquoise by sifting together the ground hazelnuts, icing sugar, and cocoa powder. Gently fold into the aquafaba meringue to combine.

Fit a large piping bag fitted with an open circle tip, and fill with the dacquoise. Following the circle outlines on the parchment paper, pipe three spiraling disks, creating three meringue disks in total.

BAKE THE MERINGUE

Bake the disks for 2 hours until crisp and dried out, then turn the oven off and let them dry further in the oven, until they cool to room temperature. Don't worry if there are cracks in your meringue disks! They'll be covered with delicious ganache and mocha buttercream. The disks can be made ahead and stored in an airtight container overnight, with parchment paper between each layer.

ASSEMBLE THE CAKE

Place the first completely cooled meringue disk on a cake board or serving platter. Working from the center, spread a generous amount of chocolate ganache out to the edges in a flat layer. Again working from the center, spread a generous amount of mocha buttercream on top of the ganache layer. Dot with fresh raspberries, gently pressing the raspberries into the buttercream. If needed, add a little more mocha buttercream on top of the raspberries to ensure the next meringue disk has something to stick to. Repeat the process for the remaining two layers.

Alternatively, to match the photo opposite and on page 166, after spreading the first layer of meringue with ganache, fit a piping bag with a large star tip and fill it with the mocha buttercream. Instead of spreading a layer of buttercream, pipe large drop stars alternating with fresh raspberries around the perimeter of the layer. Fill the center of the layer with ganache, then place the next disk on top and repeat, repeating again with the third disk.

DECORATE THE CAKE

For the top layer, fit a piping bag fitted with the open star tip of your choice, and fill with the remaining buttercream. Decorate the top of the cake with piped drop stars and more fresh raspberries and/or edible flowers, if desired.

Refrigerate the cake, covered, for a minimum of 3 hours and up to overnight, to firm up before slicing. This cake will taste freshest eaten within a day of making it, but can be stored in the fridge, covered, for up to 3 days. See page 13 for storage notes.

FANCIFUL WILDCARD CAKES 165

Pistachio Cake

- ½ cup (125ml) soy milk
- 1 tsp apple cider vinegar
- 1 cup (130g) finely ground shelled toasted pistachios (you can use a food processor for the grinding)
- 1½ cups (195g) cake flour
- 1 tsp baking powder
- ¾ tsp fine sea salt
- ½ tsp baking soda
- ½ cup (112g) unsalted plant-based butter, room temperature
- 1¼ cups (250g) granulated white sugar
- ¼ cup (60g) sour cream
- 1 tsp pure vanilla extract
- 1 tsp pistachio or almond extract

Simple Vanilla Syrup

- 1 cup (200g) granulated white sugar
- 1 cup (250ml) water
- 1 tsp pure vanilla extract (substitute almond or pistachio extract, if desired)

Filling + Frosting

- ½ recipe Strawberry Swiss Meringue Buttercream (page 132)
- Fresh strawberries, sliced raspberries, blueberries, and gooseberries (optional)
- Fresh mint (optional)
- Whole pistachios

PISTACHIO CAKE WITH STRAWBERRY SWISS MERINGUE BUTTERCREAM

MAKES ONE 9-INCH SINGLE-LAYER CAKE

Finely ground toasted pistachios sifted with cake flour gives this beautifully nutty single-layer fancy cake its flavor. Swiss meringue strawberry buttercream is then piped on top using a large multi-pronged star tip, and the whole cake is dotted with fresh berries of all kinds, along with whole pistachios and chopped sprinkled pistachios too, if you so desire. I used what I had in the fridge to decorate this cake, which included gooseberries and fresh mint. Go nuts!

MAKE THE CAKE

Preheat the oven to 350°F (175°C). Prepare a 9-inch round cake pan by spritzing it with vegetable oil and lining with a parchment paper circle, and then spritzing again to prevent sticking.

In a small bowl, mix the soy milk with the apple cider vinegar and set aside for 10 minutes to thicken. It may look a bit separated at this point, but that's normal.

In a medium bowl, whisk together the ground pistachios, cake flour, baking powder, salt, and baking soda.

In the bowl of a stand mixer fitted with the paddle attachment, beat together the butter, sugar, sour cream, vanilla extract, and pistachio or almond extract on medium speed until combined, about 30 seconds.

With the mixer turned off, add the flour mixture to the mixer and pulse to combine. Slowly pour in the soy milk mixture and mix on low speed to combine until a batter forms, 15–30 seconds.

BAKE THE CAKE

Add the batter to the prepared cake pan, using an offset spatula to level and smooth the top. Give the pan a light tap on the counter to reduce any air bubbles. Bake for 35–40 minutes, until a toothpick inserted into the center of the cake comes out with only moist crumbs.

continued

Let the cake cool completely in the pan set on top of a wire rack.

MAKE THE SIMPLE VANILLA SYRUP

Combine the sugar and water in a small saucepan set over medium-high heat, allowing the sugar to dissolve and the mixture to reduce, 5–10 minutes. Remove from the heat and stir in the vanilla extract. Let cool completely before using. The syrup can be stored in the fridge for up to 2 weeks.

ASSEMBLE THE CAKE

Remove the cooled cake from the pan. Using a pastry brush or a teaspoon, spread a generous amount of the vanilla syrup across the top of the cake.

Dollop a generous amount of strawberry buttercream onto the center of the cake. Using your small offset spatula, frost toward the edges of the cake, leaving a half-inch of bare cake around the edge.

Fit a piping bag with a large open star tip and fill the bag with the remaining buttercream. Pipe drop stars in a circle around the border of the cake, working your way inward in circles until the entire cake is covered in piped stars. Alternate between adding sliced strawberries (and any other berry you might like) and whole pistachios to the center of each drop star. Crush up some more pistachios and sprinkle on top. Decorate further with additional berries and mint, if desired.

This cake will taste freshest eaten within a day of making it, but can be stored in the fridge, covered, for up to 3 days. See page 13 for storage notes.

Cotton Candy Cake

1 cup (250ml) soy milk

¼ cup (56g) unsalted plant-based butter

¾ tsp pure vanilla extract (or 2 tsp if not using cotton candy extract)

1 tbsp cotton candy extract

5 tbsp (75ml) aquafaba (see page 8)

2 cups (400g) granulated white sugar

2 cups (280g) all-purpose flour

2 tsp baking powder

1 tsp baking soda

¾ tsp fine sea salt

¼ tsp each of pink and blue gel colors

Filling + Frosting

1 recipe Cotton Candy Buttercream (page 127)

Pink and blue gel colors

Sprinkles of your choice

COTTON CANDY CAKE WITH WATERCOLOR BUTTERCREAM

MAKES ONE 6-INCH 3-LAYER CAKE

Cotton candy always reminds me of our local city fair, bringing back sweet memories of eating sticky, sugar-spun pink beehives while we ran around lining up for rides like the truly sketchy rickety old Wooden Coaster, or the nausea-inducing Pirate Ship. Afterward, we'd drink giant icy lemonades in the hot sun and peer through the greasy window of the mini donut machine as it fried rings of dough in hot oil, with the donuts sliding into a pool of cinnamon sugar. This cotton candy watercolor cake uses cotton candy extract as its flavor component—but you could use extra pure vanilla extract instead if you can't find cotton candy flavoring. This cake is inspired wholly by the wonderful Jenna Rae Cakes! You can find their own specialty cotton candy liquid flavor in their online shop (see Resources, page 225).

MAKE THE CAKE

Preheat the oven to 325°F (165°C). Prepare three 6- × 2-inch round cake pans by spritzing them with vegetable oil and lining with parchment paper circles cut to size, and then spritzing again with oil, to prevent sticking.

In a small saucepan set over medium heat, heat the soy milk and butter until melted and stir to combine. Remove from the heat and whisk in the vanilla and cotton candy extracts.

In the bowl of a stand mixer fitted with the whisk attachment, whip the aquafaba with the sugar until soft peaks form, about 2 minutes.

In a bowl, sift together the flour, baking powder, baking soda, and salt.

With the mixer on low speed, alternate between adding small amounts of the flour mixture and the soy milk mixture, beginning and ending with the flour. To avoid overmixing, if needed, finish the batter by hand using a rubber spatula for a few more turns until completely incorporated.

Pour half the batter into another bowl. Tint one bowl of batter with rose or electric-pink gel color, and the other bowl of batter with sky-blue gel color.

BAKE THE CAKE

Divide the pink batter evenly between the prepared cake pans. Pour the blue cake batter directly on top of the pink batter. Using a chopstick, swirl the batter in a figure-8 motion to give it a marble effect. Only do this once or twice to keep the marble look intact! Give the pans a light tap on the counter to reduce any air bubbles.

continued

Bake for 23–25 minutes, or until the cakes are lightly golden around the edges, and a toothpick inserted in the center comes out with only moist crumbs.

Let the cakes cool completely in their pans set on top of wire racks.

ASSEMBLE THE CAKE

Follow the steps on pages 19–22 to fill and frost the cake, to the final frost stage, using the uncolored cotton candy buttercream. Make sure the cake has chilled in the fridge for at least 30 minutes until firm. Divide the remaining buttercream between two bowls, coloring one bowl with pink gel color and the second bowl with blue gel color.

Using an offset spatula, add smears of the blue buttercream all around the sides of the cake. Using a cake bench scraper, scrape the sides of the cake in one full turn to smooth the buttercream and remove any excess. Wipe off the offset spatula. Next, add smears of the pink color to the cake and scrape the sides of the cake again. Continue adding smears of blue buttercream and pink buttercream and scraping the sides of the cake, one or two more times (noting that the more you combine the colors, the more the cake will have shades of purple too).

Fit a piping bag with an open circle tip and fill the bag with both remaining buttercreams in the same bag, filling one side of the bag with the blue buttercream and the other with the pink. Pipe large dollops of buttercream around the top edge of the cake, then move inward and fill the entire top of the cake with cotton candy–colored dollops. Finish with your favorite sprinkles!

This cake will taste freshest eaten within a day of making it, but can be stored in the fridge, covered, for up to 3 days. See page 13 for storage notes.

OIL PAINTING OPTION WITH MERINGUE KISSES

Meringue Kisses (optional)

1 recipe Aquafaba Meringue for Swiss Meringue Buttercream (page 129) or 1 recipe Versawhip Meringue for Swiss Meringue Buttercream (page 130)

Vanilla Blackberry Cake

1¼ cups (310ml) soy milk

2 tsp apple cider vinegar

½ cup (125ml) aquafaba (see page 8)

½ cup (112g) unsalted plant-based butter, room temperature

½ cup (125ml) vegetable oil

1½ cups (300g) granulated white sugar

1 tbsp pure vanilla extract

1 tsp vanilla bean paste

3 cups (390g) cake flour

1 tbsp baking powder

½ tsp baking soda

½ tsp fine sea salt

1 cup (125g) chopped fresh blackberries

½ cup (125ml) blackberry jam (page 141) or use your favorite store-bought

Filling + Frosting

Blackberry jam (page 141) or use your favorite store-bought

1 recipe Vanilla Swiss Meringue Buttercream (page 130)

4 gel colors of your choice

ABSTRACT-PAINTED BUTTERCREAM BLACKBERRY CAKE WITH MERINGUE KISSES

MAKES ONE 7-INCH 3-LAYER CAKE

I love making abstract painted cakes because they look so beautiful and artful. Inside, blackberries streak this vanilla cake with pretty shades of purple, and they're paired with blackberry jam filling and vanilla Swiss meringue buttercream. And on the outside, the abstract buttercream technique used is much easier than one might think—all you need is a chilled cake, a few bowls of tinted buttercream in your favorite colors, and your trusty offset spatula (or a few food-only paintbrushes if you're feeling fancy). In fact, I love the abstract technique so much, you'll see two options for finishing your cake! The first has an oil painting feel using vibrant colors and meringue kisses; the second is a watercolor-style painted cake using teal and electric pink, topped with fresh whole blackberries and piped buttercream drop stars. You can choose to use all-natural food coloring or go for bright, vibrant gel colors, depending on what kind of artful vibes you're feeling.

NOTE Make the meringue kisses the night before you're baking and let them dry overnight in the oven once it has been turned off.

MAKE THE MERINGUE KISSES

Preheat the oven to 200°F (95°C). Line a baking sheet with parchment paper.

Add a tiny amount of aquafaba meringue to the underside of the parchment paper to stick down the paper to the pan. Fill a piping bag fitted with an open circle tip or open star tip with the meringue. Pipe meringue dollops or drop stars directly onto the parchment paper, experimenting with larger and smaller ones if desired, spacing them out evenly on the paper.

continued

FANCIFUL WILDCARD CAKES

Bake for 1½ hours, making sure they aren't browning, until dried out and non-sticky to the touch. Turn the oven off, and let them dry out completely overnight in the oven if you can. Leftover meringue kisses can be stored in an airtight container, layered with parchment paper, for up to 1 week.

MAKE THE CAKE

Preheat the oven to 350°F (175°C). Prepare three 7- × 2-inch round cake pans by spritzing them with vegetable oil and lining with parchment paper circles cut to size, and then spritzing again with oil, to prevent sticking.

In a small bowl, mix the soy milk with the apple cider vinegar together for about 15 seconds. Set aside for 5 minutes to thicken. It may look a bit separated at this point, but that's normal.

In a separate small bowl, whisk the aquafaba until foamy and light, about 1 minute, and set aside.

In the bowl of a stand mixer fitted with the paddle attachment, cream together the butter, vegetable oil, and sugar until creamy and well blended. Add ½ cup (125ml) of the foamy aquafaba, as well as the vanilla extract and vanilla bean paste, mixing well until combined.

In a large bowl, whisk together the cake flour, baking powder, baking soda, and salt.

With the mixer on low speed, alternate between adding the flour mixture and the soy milk mixture, beginning and ending with the flour mixture, mixing until just combined. Use a spatula to fold in any stray flour lumps, and be careful not to overmix the batter.

BAKE THE CAKE

Divide the cake batter evenly between the prepared pans. Evenly disperse the blackberries and jam over the cakes, using a chopstick to gently swirl the components together for a marbled effect. Give the pans a light tap on the counter to reduce any air bubbles.

Bake for 22–25 minutes, until the cake edges are lightly browned, and a toothpick inserted into the center comes out with only moist crumbs.

Let the cakes cool completely in their pans set on top of wire racks.

ASSEMBLE THE CAKE

Follow the steps on pages 19–22 to fill and frost the cake with some of the blackberry jam and vanilla Swiss meringue buttercream, to the final frost stage. While building the cake, follow the dugout pool method to add some extra blackberry jam to the layers. For both the cakes pictured with this recipe, I used a smooth style for the second layer of frosting.

You will need a firm, chilled cake to work on for the next stage, so you have a proper cake canvas to paint on. Power-chill the cake again in the freezer for 12–15 minutes, or in the fridge for 30 minutes or so. (If you're going to chill your cake for longer, make sure to cover it with a cake dome to keep the cake from absorbing fridge smells!) The color and style options are endless—I've included below two decorating styles to work from. Use these designs as a starting point for "painting" your cakes!

OIL PAINTING OPTION

Divide the remaining buttercream between four small bowls. Choose your favorite color palette and add a few drops of gel color to each bowl, mixing to combine. Note that the color will become more vibrant and darker as it sets, so start with a tiny amount of color and add more as needed. With gel color, less is more, as it is concentrated. For the cake pictured on page 176, I mixed royal blue, sky blue, and purple gel colors to achieve the cobalt blue shade. The second color is fuchsia; the third is a peach mixed with pink; and the fourth an avocado green.

Once your cake is chilled, place it onto a cake turntable. You'll be using a small offset spatula (or a butter knife) as your palette knife. Dip the underside of the front tip of the spatula into the first color. Place the buttercream against the cake and pull the spatula horizontally in a smearing motion, creating an oil-painting-like swoosh. Continue dipping and painting the cake in the same color, being thoughtful with placement, turning the turntable as you go. Wipe the spatula clean with a paper towel, then dip into the next buttercream color and repeat the process until the entire cake, including the top, is painted with each color.

Top with a few artfully placed meringue kisses.

WATERCOLOR OPTION

Divide the remaining buttercream between two small bowls. Choose your favorite color palette and add a few drops of gel color to each bowl, mixing to combine. For the cake pictured below, I used an electric-pink gel color and a teal gel color.

Once your cake is chilled, place it onto a cake turntable. Using an offset spatula, begin adding smears of teal buttercream to the cake. Using a cake bench scraper, scrape the buttercream in one full turn, scraping off any excess. Wipe the spatula clean with paper towel, then add smears of pink buttercream to the cake, scraping as you did the teal color. Continue adding and scraping one or two more times (noting that the more you combine the colors, the more the cake will have shades of purple).

Fit a piping bag fitted with an open star tip and fill the bag with the remaining buttercream of both colors. Pipe drop stars onto the top of the cake, alternating with fresh blackberries.

This cake will taste freshest enjoyed within a day of making it, but can be stored in the fridge, covered, for up to 3 days. See page 13 for more storage notes.

WATERCOLOR OPTION

FANCIFUL WILDCARD CAKES 179

(TO FEED A CROWD)

6

FANCY SHEET CAKES

Vanilla Sheet Cake

1 cup (250ml) soy milk

½ cup (125g) sour cream

5 tbsp (75ml) aquafaba (see page 8)

1 tbsp pure vanilla extract

3 cups (390g) cake flour

1½ cups (300g) granulated white sugar

1 tsp baking powder

¾ tsp baking soda

¾ tsp fine sea salt

1 cup (224g) unsalted plant-based butter, room temperature

Vanilla Milk Soak

1 cup (250ml) soy milk

3 tbsp granulated white sugar

1 tsp pure vanilla extract

Pinch of salt

Frosting

Raspberry jam (page 141) or use your favorite store-bought

1 recipe Vanilla Swiss Meringue Buttercream (page 130)

4 gel colors of your choice

2 dozen fresh raspberries

BUTTERCREAM FLOWER GARDEN HOLY SHEET CAKE

MAKES ONE 9- × 13-INCH SHEET CAKE

I made a version of this beautiful buttercream flower–piped "Holy Sheet Cake" for *Cherry Bombe* magazine's Jubilee Seattle conference back in late 2019—vanilla milk–soaked vanilla cake with a raspberry jam layer, topped with vanilla Swiss meringue buttercream flowers, drop stars, and leaves, and finished with fresh raspberries.

    I named it the Holy Sheet Cake at the time, and getting it frosted, piped, sliced, and individually plated for 200+ conference guests was truly a holy sheet miracle—I felt like I was living my own *Top Chef* elimination challenge, hehe. With the help of some awesome assistants, the cakes were served and I met so many wonderful folks and had the best day. I love this color blast of a cake—it's an homage to, and a celebration of, all the brilliant, dynamic, and inspiring women in food I have met through *Cherry Bombe* magazine and their community-building Jubilee conferences.

MAKE THE CAKE

Preheat the oven to 350°F (175°C). Prepare a 9- × 13-inch rectangular cake pan by spritzing it with vegetable oil and lining with a parchment paper rectangle cut to size, and then spritzing again with oil, to prevent sticking.

In a large bowl, using a balloon whisk, vigorously whisk the soy milk, sour cream, aquafaba, and vanilla extract together until combined and frothy.

In the bowl of a stand mixer fitted with the paddle attachment, mix together the cake flour, sugar, baking powder, baking soda, and salt until combined.

With the mixer on low speed, add the butter, 1-inch pieces at a time (I just use a butter knife to slice off pieces from the brick of butter right into the bowl). The mixture should clump up and look as if there are some coarse sand–like pieces in there.

With the mixer still on low, pour in half of the whipped milk mixture, mixing for about 15 seconds to incorporate. Pour in the remaining milk mixture and mix until a smooth batter forms, about 30 seconds. To avoid overmixing, if needed, finish the batter by hand using a rubber spatula for a few more turns until completely incorporated.

BAKE THE CAKE

Pour the batter into the prepared cake pan, tapping the pan on the counter a few times to reduce any air bubbles. Smooth the batter with an offset spatula, if needed. Bake for 30–34 minutes, until the cake is lightly browned on the top and edges, and a toothpick inserted into the center comes out with only moist crumbs.

Let the cake cool completely in its pan set on top of a wire rack.

MAKE THE VANILLA MILK SOAK

In a small saucepan set over medium heat, combine the soy milk, sugar, vanilla extract, and salt, stirring until the sugar has dissolved completely. Remove from the heat and let cool completely.

ASSEMBLE THE CAKE

The ease of sheet cakes is that you can serve them right in the pan they were baked in! But if you want to serve on a cake board, see the note on this page.

Using a serrated bread knife, trim off any dome from the cake, keeping the trimmings for a snack. Using a pastry brush or teaspoon, generously brush the vanilla milk soak all over the cake, using enough to impart flavor but not so much that the cake becomes mushy.

Apply a thin layer of jam on the entire cake. Using a rubber spatula, dollop enough vanilla Swiss meringue buttercream to the center of the cake to make a thin but substantial layer, then carefully spread the buttercream to the edges of the cake. Don't worry if it gets a bit mingled up with the jam, as the whole cake will be covered in colored buttercream piping!

DECORATE THE CAKE

Dot the entire cake in an even pattern with the raspberries, pressing them lightly into the buttercream.

Divide the remaining buttercream between four bowls. Tint each bowl with your favorite gel colors—I used fuchsia pink, turquoise, avocado green, and Wedgwood blue for the cake in this photo. Fit four piping bags each with a different piping tip (I used Wilton 4B for the pink and blue, Wilton 1M for the turquoise, and Wilton 70 for the avocado green), then fill each with a different color of buttercream, reserving the leaf tip for the avocado green. Pipe an assortment of different-sized drop stars and rosettes all over the cake, adding piped leaves to fill in any holes.

For neat and tidy slices, chill the cake for 30 minutes before slicing, wiping your knife clean between cuts.

This cake will taste freshest eaten within a day of making it, but can be stored in the fridge, covered, for up to 3 days. See page 13 for storage notes.

> To unmold a sheet cake from the cake pan, run an offset spatula around the edges of the cooled cake. Place a large cutting board directly on top of the cake pan. Carefully but deftly invert the cake onto the cutting board, then peel off the parchment paper. Place your cake board or a large platter on the bottom of the cake, then turn the cake right side up.

Vanilla Coconut Cake

3 cups (390g) cake flour

1¾ cups (350g) granulated white sugar

1 tbsp baking powder

¾ tsp fine sea salt

1½ cups (375ml) full-fat coconut milk

¾ cup (185ml) vegetable oil

2 tsp apple cider vinegar

2 tsp pure vanilla extract

Passion Fruit Syrup

6–7 fresh passion fruits, or ½ cup (100g) passion fruit pulp

1 cup (250ml) water

1 cup (200g) granulated white sugar

Haupia Layer

4 cups (1L) full-fat coconut milk

⅔ cup (130g) granulated white sugar

½ cup cornstarch

¼ tsp fine sea salt

Toasted Coconut

1 cup (100g) unsweetened coconut flakes or shreds

Whipped Coconut Cream

2 cups (500ml) coconut cream, refrigerated in the cans for 24 hours (see note)

½ cup (65g) icing sugar, sifted

1 tsp pure vanilla extract

Pinch of salt

Topping

Edible flowers (optional)

Pineapple triangles (optional)

COCONUT HAUPIA CAKE WITH PASSION FRUIT SYRUP

MAKES ONE 9- × 13-INCH SHEET CAKE

The magical island of Maui, Hawaii, has a special place in our family's hearts—when we can't be in the tropical, flower-fragrant air downing bowls of shave ice, we can eat our favorite Hawaiian treats by making them at home. This cake is an homage to my family's love of Hawaii—white vanilla coconut cake with passion fruit syrup and creamy coconut haupia, topped with billowy whipped coconut cream and toasted coconut, then decorated with edible flowers and little triangles of fresh pineapple, if desired.

For the passion fruit syrup, you can use fresh passion fruit (tip: they look dry and wrinkly when they're ripe!) or passion fruit puree, often found in Asian or international grocery stores; if you can't find either, passion fruit juice can be reduced to thicken and then used as the cake soak.

 NOTE This recipe requires a little planning ahead of time. You'll want to refrigerate your coconut cream cans in the fridge 24 hours before using them—the precious cream separates from the coconut water, and the cream is where it's at! Reserve the coconut water for drinking on its own, or blending into your next smoothie! The cake, once baked and cooled, also needs to be refrigerated to set overnight. Prepare the coconut whipped cream shortly before serving.

MAKE THE CAKE

Preheat the oven to 350°F (175°C). Prepare a 9- × 13-inch rectangular cake pan by spritzing it with vegetable oil, and lining with a parchment paper rectangle cut to size, and then spritzing again with oil, to prevent sticking.

continued

FANCY SHEET CAKES 187

In the bowl of a stand mixer fitted with the paddle attachment, mix together the flour, sugar, baking powder, and salt until combined.

In a medium bowl, whisk together the coconut milk, vegetable oil, apple cider vinegar, and vanilla extract.

With the mixer off, add the wet ingredients to the dry ingredients and pulse to combine without causing a dust storm. Mix on low speed to combine until a batter forms, 15–30 seconds. Do not overmix. Use a spatula to fold in any stray flour lumps, but try not to overmix the batter.

BAKE THE CAKE

Pour the batter into the prepared cake pan. Give the pan a light tap on the counter to reduce any air bubbles. Bake for 30–35 minutes, turning the pan halfway through baking time, until the edges and top are lightly browned, and a toothpick inserted into the center comes out with only moist crumbs. If the cake has a domed center, very carefully flatten it while it is still hot and malleable, using a piece of parchment paper and an oven mitt.

Let the cake cool completely in its pan set on top of a wire rack.

MAKE THE PASSION FRUIT SYRUP

If using fresh passion fruit, slice each passion fruit in half and scoop out the pulp (keep the rest of the fruit for another use). Add the pulp, water, and sugar to a small saucepan and bring to a boil over medium-high heat. Reduce the heat to low and simmer until the syrup has reduced by half. Strain the syrup into a clean, empty jar. Let cool completely and refrigerate until using.

With a teaspoon, generously spoon passion fruit syrup over the completely cooled cake, allowing it to soak in. Set the cake aside while making the haupia layer.

MAKE THE HAUPIA LAYER

In a medium saucepan set over medium-high heat, combine the coconut milk with the sugar, cornstarch, and salt. Heat, whisking continuously to dissolve the sugar and to prevent any cornstarch-related lumps, until the mixture begins to thicken, 5–7 minutes. Cook for another 5 or so minutes, until the mixture has thickened to the consistency of thick glue and can coat the back of a spoon.

Remove from the heat and pour on top of the cooled cake, still in the cake pan. Refrigerate, covered, overnight.

TOAST THE COCONUT

Preheat the oven to 350°F (175°C). Line a baking sheet with parchment paper and spread the coconut flakes onto the sheet. Bake for 8–10 minutes, until toasted and browned, tossing them halfway. Be careful not to let them burn! Remove from the oven and allow to cool completely.

MAKE THE WHIPPED COCONUT CREAM

Meanwhile, when ready to assemble the cake, place the metal bowl and whisk attachment of your stand mixer in the freezer to chill for 10–15 minutes.

Fit your stand mixer with the chilled bowl and whisk attachment and whip the coconut cream until thickened and fluffy. Add the icing sugar, vanilla extract, and pinch of salt and beat for another minute to combine. Immediately spread on top of the chilled haupia layer of the cake.

SERVE THE CAKE

Slice the cake into generous squares, adding a dollop of whipped coconut cream to each and sprinkling with toasted coconut. Decorate with edible flowers and little triangles of pineapple, if desired.

This cake will taste freshest eaten within a day of making it, but can be stored in the fridge (before it is topped with the whipped coconut cream), covered, for up to 3 days. See page 13 for storage notes.

Carrot Pineapple Cake

1 cup (200g) golden brown sugar

¾ cup (150g) granulated white sugar

½ cup (125ml) vegetable oil

1 cup (300g) canned crushed pineapple

1 cup (250ml) soy milk

2 tsp pure vanilla extract

3 cups (320g) grated carrots

1 tbsp grated fresh ginger

3 cups (420g) all-purpose flour

2 tsp ground cinnamon

2 tsp baking powder

1 tsp baking soda

1 tsp ground ginger

1 tsp fine sea salt

Frosting

1 recipe Tangy Yogurt Frosting (page 140)

CARROT PINEAPPLE SHEET CAKE WITH TANGY YOGURT FROSTING

MAKES ONE 9- × 13-INCH SHEET CAKE

Carrot cake is right up there among my favorite cakes—and this one is extra moist from shredded carrots and sweet pineapple and fragrant with flecks of ginger and cinnamon. The tangy yogurt frosting mimics a classic cream cheese frosting glaze, with its creamy citrus tang, and is dolloped on top of individual slices of cake for serving.

MAKE THE CAKE

Preheat the oven to 350°F (175°C) Prepare a 9- × 13-inch cake pan by spritzing it with vegetable oil and lining with a parchment paper rectangle cut to size, and then spritzing again with oil, to prevent sticking.

In the bowl of a stand mixer fitted with the paddle attachment, mix the brown sugar and white sugar with the vegetable oil, crushed pineapple, soy milk, vanilla extract, grated carrot, and grated ginger until combined.

In a large bowl, whisk together the flour, cinnamon, baking powder, baking soda, ground ginger, and sea salt.

With the mixer turned off, add the dry ingredients to the stand mixer, pulsing to combine, about five pulses. Turn the mixer to low speed to combine the batter, scraping down the sides of the bowl as needed, 15–20 seconds.

BAKE THE CAKE

Pour the cake batter into the prepared pan. Give the pan a light tap on the counter to reduce any air bubbles. Bake for 28–30 minutes, until the cake edges are lightly browned, the cake has puffed up slightly, and a toothpick inserted into the center comes out with only moist crumbs.

Let the cake cool completely in its pan set on top of a wire rack.

ASSEMBLE THE CAKE

Slice the cake into squares while still in the pan and plate individually. Add a generous dollop of frosting to the center of each slice, allowing the frosting to drip down the sides.

This cake will taste freshest eaten within a day of making it, but can be stored in the fridge, covered, for up to 3 days. See page 13 for storage notes.

Lemon Syrup

About 3 lemons

1 cup (200g) granulated white sugar

Lemon Coconut Cake

2 cups (400g) granulated white sugar

Zest of 4 lemons (4 tbsp approximately)

1 cup (250ml) soy milk

¼ cup (60ml) fresh lemon juice

½ cup (125ml) coconut cream

3 cups (390g) cake flour

1 tbsp baking powder

1 tsp baking soda

1 tsp fine sea salt

Frosting

1 recipe Lemon Swiss Meringue Buttercream (page 132)

Candied lemon (page 39) (optional)

LEMON COCONUT CAKE WITH LEMON SWISS MERINGUE BUTTERCREAM

MAKES ONE 9- × 13-INCH SHEET CAKE

I have a personal affinity to anything remotely tropical in flavor, and this sunny-vibes cake hits all the right notes with its lemon syrup–soaked, lemon coconut cream cake, and lemon Swiss meringue buttercream! Coconut milk has been one of my vegan champion ingredients over the years because of the way it adds richness—it's a liquid gold product, in my humble opinion—I bow down to you, humble coconut! We live close to a diverse collection of greengrocers, with their colorful displays of fresh produce lining the streets, and one of my favorite memories is the day a few years ago when Teddy saw a box of hairy brown bowling-ball coconuts as we were walking past. We brought one home, drilled it, and drank the watery, lightly sweet contents; then we cracked the remainder open with a hammer! Ah, the fruity fun discoveries of childhood!

NOTE: Make the lemon rind syrup 1 day ahead. Recipe inspired by the ingenious Stella Parks!

MAKE THE LEMON SYRUP

Juice the lemons, until you have ½ cup (125ml) fresh squeezed lemon juice. Chop up the rinds (removing the seeds first) and mix well with the sugar. Let the mixture sit for 3 hours, mixing every now and then, until the sugar is dissolved and a lemony syrup is forming. Squeeze the rinds to get all the goodness out. Mix with the lemon juice and refrigerate in a covered glass jar overnight for use the next day. Leftover lemon syrup will keep for 2 weeks in the fridge—use it to flavor a fancy bubbly water drink or icy cocktail.

MAKE THE CAKE

Preheat the oven to 350°F (175°C). Prepare a 9- × 13-inch rectangular cake pan by spritzing it with vegetable oil and lining with a parchment paper rectangle cut to size, and then spritzing again with oil, to prevent sticking.

In a small bowl, combine the sugar with the lemon zest, rubbing the lemon zest into the sugar with your fingertips until the sugar is fragrant and pale yellow.

continued

In a large bowl, whisk together the soy milk, lemon juice, and coconut cream to combine.

In a medium bowl, combine the cake flour, baking powder, baking soda, salt, and lemon sugar.

Add the dry ingredients to the wet ingredients, whisking to combine so a smooth batter forms.

BAKE THE CAKE

Pour the batter into the prepared cake pan, tapping the pan on the counter a few times to reduce any air bubbles. Smooth the batter with an offset spatula, if needed. Bake for 30–34 minutes, until the cake is lightly browned on the top and edges, and a toothpick inserted into the center comes out with only moist crumbs.

Let the cake cool completely in its pan set on top of a wire rack.

ASSEMBLE THE CAKE

Read the note on page 183 on how to unmold the cake from the pan. Using a serrated bread knife, trim off any dome from the cake, keeping the trimmings for a snack.

Using a pastry brush, generously brush the top of the cake with lemon syrup. Using an offset spatula, frost the top of the cake with a thin layer of the lemon Swiss meringue buttercream.

Fit a large piping bag with an open circle tip and fill the bag with the remaining lemon buttercream. Pipe dollops of buttercream all over the top of the cake. Decorate with candied lemon as pictured, plus you can also always add edible flowers or a sprinkling of fresh lemon zest, if desired.

This cake will taste freshest eaten within a day of making it, but can be stored in the fridge, covered, for up to 3 days. See page 13 for storage notes.

Funfetti Cake

1 cup (250ml) soy milk

1 tsp apple cider vinegar

5 tbsp (75ml) aquafaba (see page 8)

1½ cups (210g) all-purpose flour

⅔ cup (90g) cake flour

1 tsp baking soda

1 tsp baking powder

¾ tsp fine sea salt

¾ cup (180g) unsalted plant-based butter, room temperature

1¼ cups (250g) granulated white sugar

2 tsp pure vanilla extract

½ cup rainbow sprinkles (do not use naturally colored sprinkles)

Vanilla Syrup

1 cup (250ml) water

1 cup (200g) granulated white sugar

1 tsp pure vanilla extract

Frosting

1 recipe Vanilla Bean Buttercream (page 125)

Purple gel color (optional)

Assorted edible flowers

PRESSED FLOWER FUNFETTI CAKE BARS

MAKES ONE 13- × 18-INCH SHEET CAKE

Chef Heather Wong is quite possibly the cutest pastry chef ever—I've been following her for well over a decade, since back when she was known as Scootabaker (delivering cakes on a scooter around Los Angeles!). I am in love with her signature pressed-flower cake bars, so here is an homage to her amazing work, veganized for your plant-based cake enjoyment! These flower-inspired modern cake bars would be so cute for a bridal shower, birthday party, or fancy movie night.

NOTE Pressed edible flowers generally take up to 2 weeks to dry and flatten (see page 38)—so if you don't have that kind of time, power-press them for a day and you'll still be able to use them, they just won't be paper-flat! Make sure you're using certified organic edible flowers from the farmers' market, grocery store, or your own garden. I've used ruffly pansies in a myriad of colors. This cake requires a large, rimmed 13- × 18-inch baking sheet, but you can also use your trusty 9- × 13-inch cake pan to make this a single-layer sheet cake instead.

MAKE THE CAKE

Preheat the oven to 350°F (175°C). Prepare a 13- × 18-inch rectangular rimmed baking sheet by spritzing it with vegetable oil and lining with a parchment paper rectangle cut to size, and then spritzing again with oil, to prevent sticking.

In a small bowl, mix the soy milk with the apple cider vinegar and set aside for 10 minutes to thicken. It may look a bit separated at this point, but that's normal.

In a small bowl, vigorously whisk the aquafaba until frothy, about 30 seconds.

In a medium bowl, whisk together the all-purpose flour, cake flour, baking soda, baking powder, and salt until combined.

In the bowl of a stand mixer fitted with the paddle attachment, beat the butter and sugar on high speed until light and fluffy, about 2 minutes. On low speed, add the aquafaba and vanilla extract and continue beating until combined, scraping down the sides of the bowl as needed.

continued

FANCY SHEET CAKES   195

With the mixer on low speed, alternate between adding the flour mixture and soy milk mixture, mixing to combine after each addition: add one-third of the dry ingredients, followed by half of the soy milk mixture, followed by another third of the dry ingredients and the remaining soy milk, and then finish with the remaining dry ingredients, mixing 30–60 seconds in total until a smooth batter forms.

Using a rubber spatula, gently fold in the rainbow sprinkles.

BAKE THE CAKE

Pour the batter onto the prepared baking sheet, using an offset spatula to spread it evenly to the sides. Give the pan a light tap on the counter to reduce any air bubbles. Bake for 18–22 minutes, until the cake is lightly golden on top, and a toothpick inserted into the center of the cake comes out with only moist crumbs.

Let the cake cool completely in its pan set on top of a wire rack.

MAKE THE VANILLA SYRUP

In a small saucepan set over medium-high heat, heat the water and sugar until they are gently boiling and all the sugar has dissolved. Remove from the heat, stir in the vanilla extract, and let cool completely before using.

ASSEMBLE THE CAKE

Carefully remove the cake from the baking sheet (see the note on page 183) and set on a flat surface such as a large cutting board. Using a large sharp knife, cut the cake in half crosswise. Using a pastry brush, brush a generous amount of vanilla syrup onto the first layer. Stir the gel color into the vanilla bean buttercream, then spread a generous, even layer of the light purple buttercream on the top of the first layer. Place the other half of the cake on top of the buttercream, top side down, and gently press down.

Add a second brushing of vanilla syrup to the top layer of cake. Then, using an offset spatula, spread the remaining buttercream in a generous, even, and smooth layer over the top of the cake.

Place the edible flowers on top of the cake in a pleasing pattern.

Chill the cake until firm, about 30 minutes. Using a very sharp large knife heated up in hot water and then dried, trim the edges of the cakes to give you a clean cut edge for your cake bars. Slice the cake crosswise into 8 strips, then slice in half vertically to create 16 slender bars, wiping the knife clean between cuts as needed.

Assemble the cake bars on a platter or cake plate and serve.

This cake will taste freshest eaten within a day of making it, but can be stored in the fridge, covered, for up to 3 days. See page 13 for storage notes.

Raspberry Lemon Sheet Cake

1½ cups (300g) granulated white sugar

2 tbsp lemon zest

1 cup (250ml) soy milk

½ cup (112g) plant-based sour cream

¼ cup (60ml) fresh lemon juice

5 tbsp (75ml) aquafaba (see page 8)

1 tbsp pure vanilla extract

3 cups (390g) cake flour

1 tsp baking powder

¾ tsp baking soda

¾ tsp fine sea salt

1 cup (224g) unsalted plant-based butter

2 cups (250g) fresh raspberries

Frosting

1 recipe Raspberry Italian Meringue Buttercream (page 137)

2 dozen fresh raspberries

Candied lemon (page 39), cut into small pieces (optional)

RASPBERRY LEMON SHEET CAKE WITH RASPBERRY ITALIAN MERINGUE BUTTERCREAM

MAKES ONE 9- × 13-INCH SHEET CAKE

Razz + Lemon: Tangy Meets Tangy—a new sitcom? This summery sheet cake can do the rounds at just about any occasion. All of your guests will want to tuck into this soft, plush lemon cake dotted with raspberries throughout, frosted with piped raspberry Italian meringue buttercream and decorated with—you guessed it!—more fresh raspberries! If you're not feeling like whipping out the piping bag and open star tips for the decoration, feel free to frost simply with gentle swoops and swirls of buttercream instead. Easy *Razz + Lemon* times!

MAKE THE CAKE

Preheat the oven to 350°F (175°C). Prepare a 9- × 13-inch rectangular cake pan by spritzing it with vegetable oil and lining with a parchment paper rectangle cut to size, and then spritzing again with oil, to prevent sticking.

In a small bowl, combine the sugar with the lemon zest, rubbing the lemon zest into the sugar with your fingertips until the sugar is fragrant and pale yellow.

In a large bowl using a balloon whisk, vigorously whisk the soy milk, sour cream, lemon juice, aquafaba, and vanilla extract together until combined and frothy.

In the bowl of a stand mixer fitted with the paddle attachment, mix together the flour, lemon sugar, baking powder, baking soda, and salt until combined.

With the mixer on low speed, add the butter, 1-inch pieces at a time (I just use a butter knife to slice off pieces from the brick of butter right into the bowl). The mixture should clump up and look as if there are some coarse sand–like pieces in there.

With the mixer still on low, pour in half of the whipped milk mixture, mixing for about 15 seconds to incorporate. Pour in the remaining milk mixture and mix until a smooth batter forms, about 30 seconds. To avoid overmixing, if needed, finish the batter by hand using a rubber spatula for a few more turns until completely incorporated. Gently fold in 1 cup (125g) of the raspberries.

continued

BAKE THE CAKE

Pour the batter into the prepared cake pan, tapping the pan on the counter a few times to reduce any air bubbles. Smooth the batter with an offset spatula, if needed. Evenly sprinkle the remaining raspberries on top of the batter, pressing them into the batter gently.

Bake for 30–34 minutes, until the cake is lightly browned on the top and edges, and a toothpick inserted into the center comes out with only moist crumbs.

Let the cake cool completely in its pan set on top of a wire rack.

ASSEMBLE THE CAKE

The ease of sheet cakes is that you can serve them right in the pan they were baked in! If you want to serve this cake on a cake board, read the note on page 183 on how to unmold the cake from the pan.

Using a serrated bread knife, trim off any dome from the cake, keeping the trimmings for a snack.

To serve in the cake pan, apply a thin layer of the raspberry Italian meringue buttercream to the top all the way to the edges, being careful it doesn't get too messy. Fit a piping bag fitted with an open star tip—I used both the Wilton 1M and 4B for this cake—and fill the bag with the remaining buttercream. Place fresh raspberries at random on top of the cake. Pipe rosettes and drop stars of different sizes and shapes on the top of the cake and nestled next to the raspberries. Dot the cake with chopped candied-lemon pieces (page 39), if desired.

To serve on a cake board, see the note on page 183. You can choose to frost the entire cake (top and sides) with a crumb coat and final coat, as per the steps on pages 19–22. Or you can frost only the top, as in the picture on page 198.

This cake will taste freshest eaten within a day of making it, but can be stored in the fridge, covered, for up to 3 days. See page 13 for storage notes.

Tie-Dye Cake

1¼ cups (310ml) soy milk

2 tsp apple cider vinegar

½ cup (125ml) aquafaba (see page 8)

½ cup (112g) unsalted plant-based butter, room temperature

½ cup (125ml) vegetable oil

1½ cups (300g) granulated white sugar

1 tbsp pure vanilla extract

1 tsp vanilla bean paste

3 cups (390g) cake flour

1 tbsp baking powder

1 tsp baking soda

1 tsp fine sea salt

4 gel colors of your choice (such as pink, green, yellow, and turquoise)

Frosting

1½ recipes Vanilla Buttercream (page 125)

6 gel colors in your choice of rainbowy colors (such as coral, pink, yellow, green, turquoise, and violet)

TIE-DYE RAINBOW PIPED BUTTERCREAM CAKE

MAKES ONE 9- × 13-INCH SHEET CAKE

Got a Pride party coming up and need to feed a glittering, gorgeous crowd? Is your child obsessed with rainbows, *and* do they also lean toward plant-based eating? Is it your own personal unicorn's BIRTHDAY? Have I got the cake for you. Slice on into this super cool but sneakily simple tie-dye-effect cake, piped with the cutest buttercream rainbow pattern. You can use natural food color powders or natural gel colors for both the tie-dye swirled batter and buttercream piping, or you can go hyper-vibrant gel color, using all the electric shades!

MAKE THE CAKE

Preheat the oven to 350°F (175°C). Prepare a 9- × 13-inch rectangular cake pan by spritzing it with vegetable oil and lining with a parchment paper rectangle cut to size, and then spritzing again with oil, to prevent sticking.

In a small bowl, mix the soy milk with the apple cider vinegar and set aside for 10 minutes to thicken. It may look a bit separated at this point, but that's normal.

In a small bowl, whisk the aquafaba until foamy and light, about 1 minute, and set aside.

In the bowl of a stand mixer fitted with the paddle attachment, cream together the butter, vegetable oil, and sugar until creamy and blended well. Add the foamy aquafaba, vanilla extract, and vanilla bean paste, mixing until combined.

In a large bowl, whisk together the cake flour, baking powder, baking soda, and salt.

With the mixer on low speed, alternate adding the flour mixture and soy milk mixture, beginning and ending with the flour mixture, until just combined. Do not overmix. Use a spatula to fold in any stray flour lumps, but try not to overmix the batter.

Divide the batter evenly between four bowls. Place ⅛ tsp of gel color in each bowl and fold in to combine. Pour the first colored batter into the prepared pan, allowing it to spread naturally. Add the second batter on top of the first, and repeat with the final two colors. Tap the pan on the counter to spread the batters to the edges.

continued

Run a chopstick through the batters in a swirl pattern to create a tie-dye effect. Do this just one or two times, otherwise the colors may blend too much. Give the pan a light tap on the counter to reduce any air bubbles.

Bake for 30–34 minutes, until the cake is lightly browned on the top and edges, and a toothpick inserted into the center comes out with only moist crumbs.

Let the cake cool completely in its pan set on top of a wire rack.

ASSEMBLE THE CAKE

The ease of sheet cakes is that you can serve them right in the pan they were baked in! But if you want to serve on a cake board, read the note on page 183 on how to unmold the cake from the pan. Using a serrated bread knife, trim off any dome from the cake, keeping the trimmings for a snack.

Using an offset spatula, apply a thin layer of vanilla buttercream to the top of the cake, all the way to the edges, being careful it doesn't get too messy.

Divide the remaining buttercream evenly between six bowls. Place just a touch of gel color into each bowl and fold in to combine.

Fit six piping bags with the piping tips of your choice and fill each bag with a different color of buttercream. For this photo, I used four different tips to create six styles of piping: a Wilton 4B for both the shell-border style and drop stars shown in turquoise and yellow; a Wilton 1M to create both the ruffle effect shown in violet and coral, and the drop stars in violet; a large grass multi-opening tip for the green; and a large leaf tip for the pink.

Pipe your chosen styles of frosting (read about the technique for each on pages 25–28), one strip at a time, starting from the end of the cake closest to you and working your way up. Use the ROYGBIV (red-orange-yellow-green-blue-indigo-violet) rainbow pattern or whichever design you like!

This cake will taste freshest eaten within a day of making it, but can be stored in the fridge, covered, for up to 3 days. See page 13 for storage notes.

7

PARTY TIME

(OR EVERYDAY)

CUPCAKES

Vanilla Cupcakes

1½ cups (375ml) soy milk

1 tsp apple cider vinegar

2¾ cups (357g) cake flour

1½ cups (300g) granulated white sugar

2 tsp baking powder

1 tsp baking soda

1 tsp fine sea salt

½ cup (125ml) vegetable oil

1 tbsp pure vanilla extract

Frosting

1 recipe Strawberry Buttercream (page 127)

12 fresh strawberries, halved

BIRTHDAY CUPCAKES WITH STRAWBERRY FROSTING

MAKES 24 CUPCAKES

Simple to make, and delicious to taste, these vanilla cupcakes with easy strawberry frosting and rainbow sprinkles will have your birthday party all set!

MAKE THE CUPCAKES

Preheat the oven to 350°F (175°C). Line two cupcake pans with cupcake liners.

In a small bowl, mix the soy milk with the apple cider vinegar and set aside for 10 minutes to thicken. It may look a bit separated at this point, but that's normal.

In the bowl of a stand mixer fitted with the paddle attachment, mix together the flour, sugar, baking powder, baking soda, and salt until combined.

With the mixer turned off, add the soy milk mixture, vegetable oil, and vanilla extract. Mix on low speed until a smooth batter forms, 15–30 seconds, scraping down the sides of the bowl as needed.

BAKE THE CUPCAKES

Using a large retractable ice cream scoop, divide the batter evenly between the prepared cupcake liners. Bake for 18–22 minutes, until the cupcakes have a gently rounded, golden-hued dome, and a toothpick inserted into the center comes out with only moist crumbs.

Let the cupcakes cool completely in their pans set on top of wire racks.

ASSEMBLE THE CUPCAKES

Fit a piping bag with an open star tip and fill the bag with the strawberry buttercream. Pipe classic swirls or rosettes of buttercream on top of the cupcakes and top each with a halved strawberry (read more about decorating cupcakes on page 34).

These cupcakes will taste freshest eaten within a day or two of making, but they can be stored in the fridge, covered, for up to 3 days. See page 13 for storage notes. Bring to cool room temperature before serving.

Blackberry Almond Cupcakes

¾ cup (185ml) soy milk

1 tsp apple cider vinegar

2 cups (280g) all-purpose flour

½ cup (60g) extra-fine almond flour

1½ tsp baking powder

1 tsp baking soda

1 tsp fine sea salt

½ cup (112g) unsalted plant-based butter, room temperature

1 cup (200g) granulated white sugar

2 tsp lemon zest

2 cups (250g) fresh or frozen halved blackberries

Frosting

1 recipe Vanilla Buttercream (page 125)

Blackberry jam (page 141) or use your favorite store-bought

2 dozen fresh blackberries

BLACKBERRY ALMOND CUPCAKES WITH VANILLA BLACKBERRY JAM FROSTING

MAKES 24 CUPCAKES

Fragrant lemon zest, moist almond flour, and zingy blackberries make these cute little cupcakes a flavor blast winner. When topped with simple vanilla frosting dolloped with blackberry jam and a fresh blackberry, they'll gently whisper—"It's elegant yet casual party time, and we're here to make this party sing." Without the frosting, they're a perfect lunchbox treat or mid-afternoon pick-me-up. To make these ultra-simple, use your favorite store-bought blackberry jam.

MAKE THE CUPCAKES

Preheat the oven to 350°F (175°C). Line two cupcake pans with cupcake liners.

In a small bowl, mix the soy milk with the apple cider vinegar and set aside for 10 minutes to thicken. It may look a bit separated at this point, but that's normal.

In a medium bowl, whisk together the flour, almond flour, baking powder, baking soda, and salt.

In the bowl of a stand mixer fitted with the paddle attachment, beat together the butter, sugar, and lemon zest until light and fluffy, about 1 minute, scraping down sides of the bowl as needed.

With the mixer on low speed, add the dry ingredients and mix to incorporate, about 15 seconds. Stream in the soy milk mixture and mix until just combined, about 30 seconds. Scrape down the bowl as needed and beat for another 15–20 seconds until a batter has formed. Carefully fold in the halved blackberries until just combined.

BAKE THE CUPCAKES

Using a large retractable ice cream scoop, divide the batter evenly between the prepared cupcake liners. Bake for 22–25 minutes until the cupcakes are have a gently rounded, golden-hued dome, and a toothpick inserted in the center comes out with only moist crumbs.

Let the cupcakes cool completely in their pans set on top of wire racks.

ASSEMBLE THE CUPCAKES

Place a generous dollop of vanilla buttercream on top of each cupcake and, using an offset spatula, spread it out to the edges (read more about decorating cupcakes on page 34). Make a shallow section in the middle of the frosting on each and add ½ tsp blackberry jam, using your offset spatula to give it one gentle swirl in the frosting. Top each cupcake with a single blackberry.

These cupcakes will taste freshest eaten within a day or two of making, but they can be stored in the fridge, covered, for up to 3 days. See page 13 for storage notes. Bring to cool room temperature before serving.

PARTY TIME (OR EVERYDAY) CUPCAKES   **209**

Vanilla Lemon Cupcakes

1½ cups (375ml) soy milk

1 tsp apple cider vinegar

2¾ cups (357g) cake flour

1½ cups (300g) granulated white sugar

2 tsp baking powder

1 tsp baking soda

1 tsp fine sea salt

½ cup (125ml) vegetable oil

1 tbsp pure vanilla extract

1 tbsp lemon zest

Frosting

1 recipe Vanilla Buttercream (page 125) (add an extra ½ cup/65g icing sugar to make it stiffer and easier to pipe)

Gel colors of your choice (I used a pink, purple, teal, and green)

GARDEN PARTY VANILLA LEMON CUPCAKES

MAKES 24 CUPCAKES

Buttercream piped drop stars, rosettes, ruffles, and leaves give these vanilla lemon cupcakes a whimsical, floral garden party upgrade! Put the skills you learned on page 34 to the cupcake test! These are a lovely addition to any celebration—a bridal shower, birthday party, coming out party—and you can adjust the colors to fit any theme.

MAKE THE CUPCAKES

Preheat the oven to 350°F (175°C). Line two 12-cup cupcake pans with cupcake liners.

In a small bowl, mix the soy milk with the apple cider vinegar and set aside for 10 minutes to thicken. It may look a bit separated at this point, but that's normal.

In the bowl of a stand mixer fitted with the paddle attachment, mix together the flour, sugar, baking powder, baking soda, and salt until combined.

With the mixer turned off, add the soy milk mixture, vegetable oil, vanilla extract, and lemon zest. Mix on low speed until a smooth batter forms, 15–30 seconds, scraping down the sides of the bowl as needed.

BAKE THE CUPCAKES

Using a large retractable ice cream scoop, divide the batter evenly between the prepared cupcake liners. Bake for 18–22 minutes, until the cupcakes have a gently rounded, golden-hued dome, and a toothpick inserted into the center comes out with only moist crumbs.

Let the cupcakes cool completely in their pans set on top of wire racks.

TINT THE FROSTING

Divide the vanilla buttercream between four small bowls. Tint each bowl with gel color—start with just a toothpick tip's worth and add more if needed. Mix each bowl of buttercream with a small spatula or spoon to incorporate the color.

ASSEMBLE THE CUPCAKES

Fit four piping bags with the piping tips of your choice and fill each piping bag with a different-colored buttercream. Pipe an assortment of drop stars, ruffles, and leaves onto the cupcakes (read more about decorating cupcakes on page 34). Fill in any empty spots with more piped leaves.

These cupcakes will taste freshest eaten within a day or two of making, but they can be stored in the fridge, covered, for up to 3 days. See page 13 for storage notes. Bring to cool room temperature before serving.

Banana Chocolate Chip Cupcakes

1 cup (250ml) soy milk

1 tsp apple cider vinegar

3 medium super ripe bananas (375g peeled)

¾ cup (150g) brown sugar

½ cup (125ml) vegetable oil

1 tsp pure vanilla extract

2½ cups (300g) whole wheat flour

2 tsp baking powder

1 tsp baking soda

1 tsp fine sea salt

1 cup (195g) bittersweet or dark plant-based chocolate chips

Frosting

1 recipe Chocolate Ganache Frosting (page 139)

Fresh berries or sprinkles (optional)

THE "THEY DON'T KNOW THEY'RE HEALTHY" BANANA CHOCOLATE CHIP CUPCAKES

MAKES 24 CUPCAKES

I love to make these muffins for Teddy's lunchbox (and my snack attacks), and they disappear quickly in our household. Not only are they delicious, they're also a healthy double-whammy fruit and fiber situation—banana-jammed and made with whole wheat flour. And do you know what happens when you add frosting to a muffin? CUPCAKE TIME! Hence their inclusion in this chapter. These would be a great choice for a children's birthday party, frosted with whipped ganache, or even a simple Vanilla Buttercream (page 125) and a dash of naturally colored sprinkles. (And, yes, you can use all-purpose flour instead of the whole wheat if that's what you have on hand!)

MAKE THE CUPCAKES

Preheat the oven to 350°F (175°C). Line two cupcake pans with cupcake liners.

In a small bowl, mix the soy milk with the apple cider vinegar and set aside for 10 minutes to thicken. It may look a bit separated at this point, but that's normal.

In the bowl of a stand mixer fitted with the paddle attachment, blend the bananas until they become liquid. Add the brown sugar, vegetable oil, and vanilla extract and blend to combine.

In a large bowl, sift together the flour, baking powder, baking soda, and salt.

With the mixer turned off, add the dry ingredients, then turn it to very low speed to gently incorporate. Stream in the soy milk mixture and mix until combined and no dry streaks remain, 15–30 seconds. Add the chocolate chips and mix on low for 15 seconds to incorporate.

BAKE THE CUPCAKES

Using a large retractable ice cream scoop, divide the batter evenly between the prepared cupcake liners. Bake for 20–22 minutes, until the cupcakes have a gently rounded, golden-hued dome, and a toothpick inserted into the center comes out with only moist crumbs.

Let the cupcakes cool completely in their pans set on top of wire racks.

continued

ASSEMBLE THE CUPCAKES

Place a dollop of chocolate ganache frosting on top of each cupcake and, using an offset spatula, spread it out to the edges (read more about decorating cupcakes on page 34). Top with a fresh berry or sprinkles, if desired.

These cupcakes will taste freshest eaten within a day or two of making, but they can be stored in the fridge, covered, for up to 3 days. See page 13 for storage notes. Bring to cool room temperature before serving.

Chocolate Chip Cupcakes

1¼ cups (310ml) soy milk

2 tsp apple cider vinegar

⅓ cup (100g) plant-based sour cream

½ cup (125ml) aquafaba (see page 8)

1 tbsp pure vanilla extract

2¾ cups (385g) all-purpose flour

1½ cups (300g) granulated white sugar

1 tbsp baking powder

1 tsp baking soda

1 tsp fine sea salt

½ cup (112g) unsalted plant-based butter

2 cups (350g) best-quality semisweet plant-based chocolate chips

Frosting

1 recipe Vanilla Buttercream (page 125) (add an extra ½ cup/65g icing sugar to make it stiffer and easier to pipe)

1 cup (175g) plant-based chocolate chips or chopped plant-based chocolate

CHOCOLATE CHIP CUPCAKES

MAKES 24 CUPCAKES

Back in the 1990s (ahem), my old high school had a canteen that busted open at recess, when you would have a quick 15 minutes to spend your measly quarters or greasy dollar bills buying a bag of chips and a carton of milk to glug down before class started again. Grade 8 HIGHLIGHT: there would also be freshly baked chocolate chip muffins. Tiny, glistening, still-melty chocolate chips studding a big ol' white vanilla (vanillin?) cake muffin. These muffins were baked by the cooking class teens, who ran the cafeteria, but sold by the school sweatsuit-wearing jocks who ran the canteen. Looking back, I wish I had taken the cafeteria cooking class, but I was probably too busy playing volleyball, or typing up notes as the student council secretary like a mega-dork.

 Instead of semisweet chocolate chips, you can use any type of bitter or dark chocolate chips or chopped chocolate.

MAKE THE CUPCAKES

Preheat the oven to 350°F (175°C). Line two cupcake pans with cupcake liners.

In a large bowl using a balloon whisk, vigorously whisk the soy milk, apple cider vinegar, sour cream, aquafaba, and vanilla extract together until combined and frothy.

In the bowl of a stand mixer fitted with the paddle attachment, mix together the flour, sugar, baking powder, baking soda, and salt until combined.

With the mixer on low speed, add the butter, 1-inch pieces at a time (I just use a butter knife to slice off pieces from the brick of butter right into the bowl). The mixture should clump up and look as if there are some coarse sand–like pieces in there.

With the mixer still on low, pour in half of the whipped milk mixture, mixing for about 15 seconds to incorporate. Pour in the remaining milk mixture and mix until a smooth batter forms, about 30 seconds. With the mixer on low speed, add the chocolate chips and mix for 15 seconds to incorporate.

continued

PARTY TIME (OR EVERYDAY) CUPCAKES   215

BAKE THE CUPCAKES

Using a large retractable ice cream scoop, divide the batter evenly between the prepared cupcake liners. Bake for 20–22 minutes until the cupcakes have a gently rounded, golden-hued dome, and a toothpick inserted in the center comes out with only moist crumbs.

Let the cupcakes cool completely in their pans set on top of wire racks.

ASSEMBLE THE CUPCAKES

Fit a piping bag with an open star tip, and fill the bag with the vanilla buttercream. Pipe a classic cupcake swirl on top of each cupcake and sprinkle with chocolate chips (read more about decorating cupcakes on page 34).

These cupcakes will taste freshest eaten within a day or two of making, but they can be stored in the fridge, covered, for up to 3 days. See page 13 for storage notes. Bring to cool room temperature before serving.

Chocolate Cupcakes

2½ cups (350g) all-purpose flour

2 cups (400g) granulated white sugar

1½ cups (180g) Dutch-process cocoa powder

2½ tsp baking soda

1¼ tsp baking powder

1 tsp fine sea salt

2 cups (500ml) full-fat coconut milk

½ cup + 2 tbsp (155ml) vegetable oil

2 tsp apple cider vinegar

2 tsp pure vanilla extract

Frosting

1 recipe Peanut Butter Frosting (page 127)

Rainbow sprinkles (optional)

1 recipe Peanut Butter Cup Crunch (page 107) (optional)

CHOCOLATE CUPCAKES WITH PEANUT BUTTER FROSTING

MAKES 24 CUPCAKES

Chocolate and peanut butter cuppies will make everything better. Rough day at the office? Long day at school? That time of the month? Stuff your face with these cupcakes. They are moist one-bowl dark chocolate cupcakes with easy peanut buttercream that will make you feel like you're winning again (and if you're feeling a little more ambitious, you could also top this with Peanut Butter Cup Crunch, page 107).

 For the peanut butter, you'll achieve the best buttercream results using the commercial, ultra-smooth kind.

MAKE THE CUPCAKES

Preheat the oven to 350°F (175°C). Line two cupcake pans with cupcake liners.

In the bowl of a stand mixer fitted with the paddle attachment, mix together the flour, sugar, cocoa powder, baking soda, baking powder, and salt on low speed until combined.

In a large bowl, whisk together the coconut milk, vegetable oil, apple cider vinegar, and vanilla extract.

With the mixer on low speed, pour the wet ingredients into the dry and mix to combine, no more than 30 seconds. If needed, finish mixing the batter by hand using a rubber spatula so it's smooth and lump-free.

BAKE THE CUPCAKES

Using a large retractable ice cream scoop, divide the batter evenly between the prepared cupcake liners. Bake for 18–22 minutes, until the cupcakes have a gently rounded, golden-hued dome, and a toothpick inserted into the center comes out with only moist crumbs.

Let the cupcakes cool completely in their pans set on top of wire racks.

ASSEMBLE THE CUPCAKES

Fit a piping bag with an open star tip, such as a Wilton 1M, and fill the bag with peanut buttercream. Pipe a classic cupcake swirl on top of each cupcake and sprinkle generously with rainbow sprinkles or peanut butter cup crunch (read more about decorating cupcakes on page 34).

These cupcakes will taste freshest eaten within a day or two of making, but they can be stored in the fridge, covered, for up to 3 days. See page 13 for storage notes. Bring to cool room temperature before serving.

Chocolate Cupcakes

1 cup (250ml) soy milk

1 tsp apple cider vinegar

2 cups (280g) all-purpose flour

1¾ cups (350g) granulated white sugar

¾ cup (90g) Dutch-process cocoa powder

2 tsp baking powder

1½ tsp baking soda

1 tsp fine sea salt

¾ cup (185ml) vegetable oil

2 tsp pure vanilla extract

½ cup (125ml) strong, hot coffee

1 cup (175g) chopped plant-based chocolate

Frosting

1 recipe Chocolate Buttercream (page 125)

Rainbow sprinkles or chocolate chips (optional)

CHOCOLATE PARTY TIME CUPCAKES

MAKES 24 CUPCAKES

Sometimes you just need a chocolate-on-chocolate situation, ideally handheld so you can quickly unwrap and direct-cram it into the mouth. To the rescue: this easy dark chocolate cupcake recipe, with a very simple chocolate frosting.

MAKE THE CUPCAKES

Preheat the oven to 350°F (175°C). Line two cupcake pans with cupcake liners.

In a small bowl, mix the soy milk with the apple cider vinegar and set aside for 10 minutes to thicken. It may look a bit separated at this point, but that's normal.

In a medium bowl, whisk to combine the flour, sugar, cocoa powder, baking powder, baking soda, and salt until mixed.

In the bowl of a stand mixer fitted with the paddle attachment, mix together the vegetable oil, vanilla extract, and soy milk mixture.

With the mixer turned off, add the dry ingredients to the wet. Turn the mixer to low speed and mix until just combined, about 15 seconds. Pour in the coffee and mix until incorporated and a batter forms, 15–30 seconds, scraping down the sides of the bowl as needed. Fold in the chopped chocolate

BAKE THE CUPCAKES

Using a large retractable ice cream scoop, divide the batter evenly between the prepared cupcake liners. Bake for 18–22 minutes, until the cupcakes have a gently rounded, golden-hued dome, and a toothpick inserted into the center comes out with only moist crumbs.

Let the cupcakes cool completely in their pans set on top of wire racks.

ASSEMBLE THE CUPCAKES

Fit a piping bag with an open star tip and fill the bag with chocolate buttercream. Pipe a classic cupcake swirl on top of each cupcake (read more about decorating cupcakes on page 34). Or, place a generous dollop of chocolate buttercream in the center of each cupcake and, using an offset spatula, work it out to the edges. Finish with sprinkles for an instant party feel or keep it casual with a single chocolate chip!

These cupcakes will taste freshest eaten within a day or two of making, but they can be stored in the fridge, covered, for up to 3 days. See page 13 for storage notes. Bring to cool room temperature before serving.

ACKNOWLEDGEMENTS

Thank you to my agent, Adrienne Rosado at Stonesong, for all your support and advice, and for putting this book into motion! Also, for allowing me to bounce many ideas off you (ahem, *Existential Cakes* still needs a publisher, hehe).

Thank you to Lindsay Paterson and Whitney Millar at Appetite Random House for the many hours of hard work in getting *Plantcakes* to fruition! It was a pleasure working with you both, and I so appreciated the honest feedback, suggestions, and shaping of this book. Many thanks also to Robert McCullough for believing in the book, and the entire team at Appetite for your diligence. Huge, in-awe thanks to Jen Griffiths for the beautiful book design—your design has encapsulated everything I could ever dream of, and reflects the fun and playful vibe of the book so lovingly! Many thanks also to Rachel Korinek, for being my off-camera flash guru, for being stupendously talented with photo editing, and for your generous, sharing nature.

To my wonderful husband, Rich—Richard's Treat! You teach me every day to be a better, kinder, and more generous person. You keep me laughing, and you're always there to support me whether it's through your words or actions or helping me practice bass lines, hehe. Thank you for everything you do for Teddy and me. Love you even MORE than a Chinese pumpkin loves a freshly baked chocolate chip cookie!

To my sweet son, Teddy—you have grown into such a kind, loving, smart, funny (and handsome!) kid. You make me so proud. Keep looking on the bright side of life and seeing the good and positivity in the world! Love you × infinity × a million × forever and a secret message—mongoose ween! Haha.

To my wonderful mom and dad—the original posicore duo! You both lead by example in being kind, thoughtful, loving, generous, and empathetic people. Thank you for your endless support through my entire life, and for being the best parents one could ever hope for! Love you both so much!

To my sisters, Leanne and Shelley—best sisters EVER! Really don't know what I'd do without you. Thank you for all of your support through my whole life. Love you!

To my wonderful mother-in-law, Beth, aka Mom T. I couldn't ask for a better mother-in-law and someone whom I love spending time with. Thank you for everything you do for us! Love you lots.

To my nephews and nieces: Brody, Kensie, Tanner, Piper, Brookie, and Sydney! Follow your dreams! Auntie Lyndsay will be by your side cheering you on.

To my extended family, aunties, cousins, and in-laws—I'm just so lucky to have the most awesome family, including all my hilarious cousins whom I adore.

To my Auntie Cor—thank you for being a special part of my life!

To my amazing friends: Amber, Sharon, Shira, Toni, Heather, Amy, Ashley, Jamie, Erika, Tara, Christa, Cindy, Miko, Becky, Mia, Yani, Erin B., Kaleb, Rebecca, my KCAR bandmates Jenni and Fiona—and too many more to mention—I am very lucky to have so many great friends and folks in my life!

Thank you to my wonderful blogging buddies for many years of friendship and support—the internet can still be a neat-o place, thanks especially to Steph, Tessa, Cynthia, Camilla, and Alana. Thank you, *Cherry Bombe* magazine (Kerry, Donna, etc.!) for being so dang cool and supportive all these years. I also want to thank my veggie friends who inspire me to create plant-based recipes and eat more consciously every day, and for their ongoing support and encouragement—Sharon Buchanan, Shira Blustein, Miko Hoffman, Erin Ireland, Sophie MacKenzie, and Desiree Nielsen. Thank you also to Brittany May Cakes for introducing me to Versawhip!

Huge love and thanks, also, to Camilla, Desiree, Erin, Kat, Kerry, and Molly for the positive support and lovely book blurbs!

Thank you, Stephanie Chan, for the author photo and for being a sweet pal and honorary cousin over many years.

To the delightful followers of the *Coco Cake Land* blog and social media, you folks are awesome. Thanks for sticking around all these years and for appreciating my "Why Be Normal?!" attitude toward cakes and life. To my wonderful cake clients past and present, thank you for the support in the beginning and for continuing to follow along on the *Coco Cake Land* journey!

To my family doctor, Dr. Winnie Su, who saved my life with an early diagnosis of breast cancer in 2015, and who delivered all of my and my sisters' babies—our whole family is very blessed to have you in our lives as our doctor and friend.

Finally, thank you to my grade four teacher, Mrs. Laurel Gurnsey. It's so amazing to me that we are now friends and writing colleagues over thirty years later. I treasure our friendship. Thank you for continuing to be my favorite teacher ever, and for your love and encouragement through all these years!

RESOURCES

EQUIPMENT

FAT DADDIO'S: Sturdy and long-lasting cake pans in every size. fatdaddios.com

KITCHENAID: For heavy-duty stand mixers that will truly last a lifetime. Buy it once, love it for life! kitchenaid.com

SCOOP N SAVE: The Canadian resource for all cake-related items—piping bags, piping tips, cake boards, gel color, edible paint. scoop-n-save.com

WILTON: The OG resource for truly all of your cake decorating needs! wilton.com

INGREDIENTS

ANITA'S COCONUT YOGURT: Organic yogurt alternative made with coconut milk. anitas.com

BECEL: Commercial brand of unsalted plant based-butter sticks. becel.com

BONNE MAMAN: My favorite store-bought jam! I horde these adorable gingham-patterned-capped jars and the delicious jam within! bonnemaman.us

BOB'S RED MILL: A trusted source for many great products—everything from baking powder to potato starch, as well as gluten-free flour. bobsredmill.com

CALLEBAUT CHOCOLATE: Dark Semisweet 811 NV or Dark Bittersweet 70–30–38NV are my plant-based go-tos for rich, deep, high-quality chocolate frostings, cakes, and cookies. callebaut.com

EARTH BALANCE: Vegan buttery sticks that are great for cakes, frostings, and cookies. earthbalancenatural.com

FLORA: Unsalted, additive-free butter, perfect for your vegan baking needs. flora.com

GUITTARD CHOCOLATE: A family- and female-run artisan chocolate company making beautiful quality chocolate wafers, chocolate baking bars, and chocolate chips. Your chocolate chip cookies will never be the same. guittard.com

INDIA TREE: Another source for natural food coloring and sprinkles. indiatree.com

JENNA RAE CAKES: They make the best cotton candy extract and other custom liquid extract flavors, all in adorable packaging. jennaraecakes.com

MIYOKO'S CREAMERY: Organic vegan butter made from cashews and coconut oil. miyokos.com

RODELLE KITCHEN: Home of high-quality fair-trade organic pure vanilla extract, vanilla beans, and organic cocoa powder. I've been using Rodelle products happily for many years. rodellekitchen.com

SPECTRUM ORGANICS VEGETABLE SHORTENING: A great-quality high-ratio shortening used in frostings and buttercreams. spectrumorganics.com

SUNCORE FOODS: Supercolor powders for coloring your cakes and frostings vibrantly and naturally using fruit and vegetables. suncorefoods.com

SWEETAPOLITA: For vegan sprinkles in both rainbow and natural colors, these are my favorite fancy sprinkles, and they will elevate all of your cakes. sweetapolitashop.com

TOFUTTI: Cream cheese and sour cream. tofutti.ca, tofutti.com

VANILLA FOOD COMPANY: Shipping to Canada and the US, they carry everything from vanilla beans to artisan quality chocolate such as Callebaut for frostings and ganaches. vanillafoodcompany.ca

VERSAWHIP: Modified soy protein powder perfect for whipping up meringues. Can be found online at modernistpantry.com (US), qualifirst.com (Canada), and through Amazon.

YOGGU! (CANADA): Thick, creamy, delicious cultured coconut yogurt. yoggu.ca

STYLING
BANQUET WORKSHOP: Hand-printed modern patterned linens, greetings cards, art prints, and even clothing. Our home is filled with their work! banquetworkshop.com

DUSEN DUSEN: Colorful linens and towels. dusendusen.com

FOOD52 SHOP: For modern, beautiful ceramic plates and everything you covet! food52.com

MEG HUBERT CERAMICS: Custom ceramic ware, from speckly mugs to pink plates! Meg has custom-made me cake platters and dessert plates, and I love all her work. meghubert.com

MY LITTLE DAY: French brand of the cutest party supplies, from paper plates and napkins to cups and party decor. mylittleday.fr

POKETO: I love the bright colors and modern patterns. Poketo is an LA-based design team creating colorful and design-conscious tableware and linens. poketo.com

XENIA TALER: Modern designs and sustainable, lightweight bamboo plates—your cake slices will look extra cute on them, and you can wash them for use again and again. xeniataler.com

INDEX

A

almond flour
  Blackberry Almond Cupcakes with Vanilla Blackberry Jam Frosting, 208–209
  Chocolate Almond Brownie Cake with Vanilla Buttercream, 47–48
  Vanilla Almond Raspberry Cake with Vanilla Buttercream + Caramel Almond Brittle, 73–74
almonds: Caramel Almond Brittle, 73–74
apples
  Apple Caramel Cake with Oatmeal Cookie Crumbles, 83–84
  Apple Olive Oil Cake with Maple Cream Cheese Frosting, 42
applesauce, as ingredient, 9
aquafaba
  Aquafaba Meringue for Italian Buttercream, 135
  Aquafaba Meringue for Swiss Meringue Buttercream, 129–130
  as ingredient, 5
  uses for, 8–9

B

baking see also decorating
  plant-based ingredients, 5–9
  storing leftovers, 13
  tips for, 15–16
  tools for, 11–12
bananas
  Banana Cake with Peanut Butter Frosting, 69
  Banana Caramel Cake with Salted Caramel Buttercream + Caramel Drips, 85–86
  as ingredient, 9
  The "They Don't Know They're Healthy" Banana Chocolate Chip Cupcakes, 213–214
bars: Pressed Flower Funfetti Cake Bars, 195–196
berries see also specific berries
  You Got Jammed (A Very Berry Quick Jam Recipe), 141
Birthday Cake Crumbles, 91–92
Birthday Cupcakes with Strawberry Frosting, 207
Black Sesame Brittle Cake with Coconut Swiss Meringue Buttercream, 159–160
blackberries
  Blackberry Almond Cupcakes with Vanilla Blackberry Jam Frosting, 208–209
  Blackberry Maple Breakfast Cake with Maple Coconut Whipped Cream, 45–46
  Abstract-Painted Buttercream Blackberry Cake with Meringue Kisses, 177–179
  You Got Jammed (A Very Berry Quick Jam Recipe), 141
blueberries
  Blueberry Sour Cream Streusel Cake, 55–56
  Fancy Breakfast Cake with Maple Italian Meringue Buttercream, Coffee Syrup + Blueberry Jam, 149–150
  You Got Jammed (A Very Berry Quick Jam Recipe), 141
brittles
  Black Sesame, 159–160
  Caramel Almond, 73–74
butter, plant-based, as ingredient, 5
Buttercream Flower Garden Holy Sheet Cake, 182–183
buttercreams, classic
  Chocolate, 125
  Chocolate Fudge, 126
  Cotton Candy, 127
  Peanut Butter Frosting, 127
  Pink Vanilla Frosting, 127
  Salted Caramel, 126
  Strawberry, 127
  Vanilla, 125
  Vanilla Bean, 125
buttercreams, Italian meringue
  Lemon, 137
  Maple, 137
  Raspberry, 137
  Vanilla, 136
buttercreams, Swiss meringue
  Chocolate, 131
  Coconut, 132
  Coffee, 131
  Lemon, 132
  Mocha, 133
  Passion Fruit Vanilla, 132
  Peanut Butter, 131
  Raspberry, 131
  Strawberry, 132
  Vanilla, 130

C

Candied Hazelnuts, 115–116
caramel
  Apple Caramel Cake with Oatmeal Cookie Crumbles, 83–84
  Banana Caramel Cake with Salted Caramel Buttercream + Caramel Drips, 85–86
  Fudgy Caramel Frosting, 139
  Passion Fruit Vanilla Bean Ombré Cake with Caramel Crunch, 89–90
  Peanut Butter Cake with Caramel Frosting, 61–62
  Salted Caramel, 126
  Salted Caramel Buttercream, 126
  Vanilla Almond Raspberry Cake with Vanilla Buttercream + Caramel Almond Brittle, 73–74
Carrot Pineapple Sheet Cake with Tangy Yogurt Frosting, 191
chocolate, plant-based
  Banana Caramel Cake with Salted Caramel Buttercream + Caramel Drips, 85–86
  Chocolate Almond Brownie Cake with Vanilla Buttercream, 47–48

Chocolate Bark, 155–157
Chocolate Chip Cupcakes, 215–216
Chocolate Fudge Buttercream, 126
Chocolate Ganache Frosting, 139
Chocolate Hazelnut Filling, 115–116
Chocolate Party Time Cupcakes, 220
Chocolate Swiss Meringue Buttercream, 131
Giant Chocolate Chip Cookie Cake with Vanilla Buttercream, 145–146
as ingredient, 5
Mocha Swiss Meringue Buttercream, 133
Peanut Butter Cup Crunch, 107–108
The "They Don't Know They're Healthy" Banana Chocolate Chip Cupcakes, 213–214

citrus: Easy Candied Citrus, 39

cocoa powder
Chocolate Almond Brownie Cake with Vanilla Buttercream, 47–48
Chocolate Buttercream, 125
Chocolate Cupcakes with Peanut Butter Frosting, 219
Chocolate Fudge Buttercream, 126
Chocolate Hazelnut Cake with Candied Hazelnuts, 115–116
Chocolate Party Time Cupcakes, 220
Cookies and Cream Cake, 101–102
Dark Chocolate Cake with Chocolate Fudge Buttercream, 78
Easy Chocolate Cake with Chocolate Ganache Frosting, 110
Holiday Vibes Chocolate Stump Cake, 155–157
Mocha Dacquoise Cake, 164–165
Party Time Chocolate Raspberry Ruffle Cake, 112–114
PB+J Chocolate Cake with Peanut Butter Cup Crunch, 107–108

coconut: Toasted Coconut, 187–188

coconut cream
Black Sesame Brittle Cake with Coconut Swiss Meringue Buttercream, 159–160
Coconut Swiss Meringue Buttercream, 132
Coconut Whipped Cream, 52

Lemon Coconut Cake with Lemon Swiss Meringue Buttercream, 193–194
Maple Coconut Whipped Cream, 45–46
Whipped Coconut Cream, 187–188

coconut milk
Coconut Haupia Cake with Passion Fruit Syrup, 187–188
as ingredient, 6

coffee
Coffee Milk Cake with Coffee Swiss Meringue Buttercream + Raspberries, 105–106
Coffee Swiss Meringue Buttercream, 131
Fancy Breakfast Cake with Maple Italian Meringue Buttercream, Coffee Syrup + Blueberry Jam, 149–150
Mocha Dacquoise Cake, 164–165
Mocha Swiss Meringue Buttercream, 133
Party Time Chocolate Raspberry Ruffle Cake, 112–114
PB+J Chocolate Cake with Peanut Butter Cup Crunch, 107–108
Vanilla Cake with Coffee Icing Glaze, 63–64

colorings, in cake making, 6

cookies
Cookies and Cream Cake, 101–102
Giant Chocolate Chip Cookie Cake with Vanilla Buttercream, 145–146
Matcha Cookie/Mini Cookies/ Crumble, 161–162
Oatmeal Cookie Crumbles, 83–84
Cotton Candy Buttercream, 127
Cotton Candy Cake with Watercolor Buttercream, 171–172
Cozy Pumpkin Pie Cake, 52
cream cheese: Maple Cream Cheese Frosting, 140

creams
Coconut Whipped, 52
Maple Coconut Whipped, 45–46
Whipped Coconut, 187–188

crumbles
Birthday Cake, 91–92
Matcha Cookie/Mini Cookies, 161–162

Oatmeal Cookie, 83–84

cupcakes
Birthday Cupcakes with Strawberry Frosting, 207
Blackberry Almond Cupcakes with Vanilla Blackberry Jam Frosting, 208–209
Chocolate Chip Cupcakes, 215–216
Chocolate Cupcakes with Peanut Butter Frosting, 219
Chocolate Party Time Cupcakes, 220
decorating tips for, 34
Garden Party Vanilla Lemon Cupcakes, 210
The "They Don't Know They're Healthy" Banana Chocolate Chip Cupcakes, 213–214

D

Dance Like No One is Watching Earl Grey Cake with Lemon Italian Meringue Buttercream, 151–152
Dark Chocolate Cake with Chocolate Fudge Buttercream, 78
decorating *see also* baking
cupcakes, 34
filling and frosting cakes, 19–22
finishing touches, 37–38
fondant, 33
piping bag tips, 25
piping styles, 26–30
tools for, 11–12

E

Earl Grey Cake, Dance Like No One is Watching, with Lemon Italian Meringue Buttercream, 151–152
Earl Grey Tea Syrup, 151–152
Easy Candied Citrus, 39
Easy Chocolate Cake with Chocolate Ganache Frosting, 110
eggs, plant-based substitutions for, 8–9
espresso *see* coffee

F

Fancy Breakfast Cake with Maple Italian Meringue Buttercream, Coffee Syrup + Blueberry Jam, 149–150

fillings
    Chocolate Hazelnut Filling, 115–116
    how to fill cakes, 19–21
finishing touches, 37–38
flavorings, in cake making, 6
flax, as egg substitute, 9
flours, in cake making, 6
flowers
    as ingredient, 6, 38
    Pressed Flower Funfetti Cake Bars, 195–196
    Vanilla Fruit + Flowers Cake with Vanilla Bean Swiss Meringue Buttercream, 95–96
fondant, and cake decorating, 33
frostings *see also* glazes; syrups
    Chocolate Buttercream, 125
    Chocolate Fudge Buttercream, 126
    Chocolate Ganache Frosting, 139
    Chocolate Swiss Meringue Buttercream, 131
    Coconut Swiss Meringue Buttercream, 132
    Coffee Swiss Meringue Buttercream, 131
    Cotton Candy Buttercream, 127
    Fudgy Caramel Frosting, 139
    how to frost cakes, 19–22
    Lemon Italian Meringue Buttercream, 137
    Lemon Swiss Meringue Buttercream, 132
    Maple Cream Cheese Frosting, 140
    Maple Italian Meringue Buttercream, 137
    Mocha Swiss Meringue Buttercream, 133
    Passion Fruit Vanilla Swiss Meringue Buttercream, 132
    Peanut Butter Frosting, 127
    Peanut Butter Swiss Meringue Buttercream, 131
    Pink Vanilla Frosting, 127
    Raspberry Italian Meringue Buttercream, 137
    Raspberry Swiss Meringue Buttercream, 131
    Salted Caramel Buttercream, 126
    Strawberry Buttercream, 127
    Strawberry Swiss Meringue Buttercream, 132
    Tangy Yogurt Frosting, 140
    Vanilla Bean Buttercream, 125
    Vanilla Buttercream, 125
    Vanilla Italian Meringue Buttercream, 136
    Vanilla Swiss Meringue Buttercream, 130
fruit *see also specific fruits*
    as ingredient, 6, 38
    Vanilla Fruit + Flowers Cake with Vanilla Bean Swiss Meringue Buttercream, 95–96
Fudgy Caramel Frosting, 139
funfetti
    Funfetti Cake with Vanilla Buttercream and Birthday Cake Crumbles, 91–92
    Pressed Flower Funfetti Cake Bars, 195–196

G

ganaches: Chocolate Ganache Frosting, 139
Garden Party Vanilla Lemon Cupcakes, 210
garnishes
    Birthday Cake Crumbles, 91–92
    Black Sesame Brittle, 159–160
    Candied Hazelnuts, 115–116
    Caramel Crunch, 89–90
    Chocolate Bark, 155–157
    Easy Candied Citrus, 39
    Matcha Cookie/Mini Cookies/Crumble, 161–162
    Meringue Kisses, 177–179
    Meringue Mushrooms, 155–156
    Oatmeal Cookie Crumbles, 83–84
    Peanut Butter Cup Crunch, 107–108
    Pistachio Cookie Moss, 155–157
    Streusel, 55–56
    Toffee Bits, 151–152
    Toffee Crunch, 85–86
Giant Chocolate Chip Cookie Cake with Vanilla Buttercream, 145–146
glazes *see also* frostings; syrups
    Coffee Icing, 63–64
    Orange Juice, 57–58
    Vanilla Bean, 51

H

hazelnuts
    Chocolate Hazelnut Cake with Candied Hazelnuts, 115–116
    Mocha Dacquoise Cake, 164–165
    Holiday Vibes Chocolate Stump Cake, 155–157

I

icing *see* buttercreams
ingredients, plant-based, 5–9
Italian meringue buttercreams *see* buttercreams, Italian meringue

J

jam
    as ingredient, 6
    You Got Jammed (A Very Berry Quick Jam Recipe), 141

L

layer cakes *see* three-layer cakes; two-layer cakes
leftovers
    storing, 13
    uses for, 16
lemons
    Dance Like No One is Watching Earl Grey Cake with Lemon Italian Meringue Buttercream, 151–152
    Easy Candied Citrus, 39
    Garden Party Vanilla Lemon Cupcakes, 210
    Lemon Coconut Cake with Lemon Swiss Meringue Buttercream, 193–194
    Lemon Italian Meringue Buttercream, 137
    Lemon Loaf Cake with Vanilla Bean Glaze, 51
    Lemon Swiss Meringue Buttercream, 132
    Lemon Syrup, 193–194
    Raspberry Lemon Sheet Cake with Raspberry Italian Meringue Buttercream, 199–200

M

maple syrup

Apple Olive Oil Cake with Maple Cream Cheese Frosting, 42
Blackberry Maple Breakfast Cake with Maple Coconut Whipped Cream, 45–46
Fancy Breakfast Cake with Maple Italian Meringue Buttercream, Coffee Syrup + Blueberry Jam, 149–150
Maple Cream Cheese Frosting, 140
Maple Italian Meringue Buttercream, 137
Matcha Green Tea Cake with Raspberry Swiss Meringue Buttercream + Matcha Mini Cookies, 161–162
Matcha Syrup, 161–162
meringues
 Aquafaba Meringue for Italian Buttercream, 135
 Aquafaba Meringue for Swiss Meringue Buttercream, 129–130
 Meringue Kisses, 177–179
 Meringue Mushrooms, 155–156
 Mocha Dacquoise Cake, 164–165
 Versawhip Meringue for Italian Buttercream, 136
 Versawhip Meringue for Swiss Meringue Buttercream, 130
milk, plant-based, as ingredient, 6
Mocha Dacquoise Cake, 164–165
Mocha Swiss Meringue Buttercream, 133

N

nuts *see also* almond flour; almonds; hazelnuts; peanut butter; peanuts; pistachios
 as ingredient, 7

O

Oatmeal Cookie Crumbles, 83–84
Orange Citrus Cake with Orange Juice Glaze, 57–58
Oreo cookies: Cookies and Cream Cake, 101–102

P

Abstract-Painted Buttercream Blackberry Cake with Meringue Kisses, 177–179

passion fruit
 Coconut Haupia Cake with Passion Fruit Syrup, 187–188
 Passion Fruit Syrup, 89–90, 187–188
 Passion Fruit Vanilla Bean Ombré Cake with Caramel Crunch, 89–90
 Passion Fruit Vanilla Swiss Meringue Buttercream, 132
peanut butter
 Banana Cake with Peanut Butter Frosting, 69
 Chocolate Cupcakes with Peanut Butter Frosting, 219
 PB+J Chocolate Cake with Peanut Butter Cup Crunch, 107–108
 Peanut Butter Frosting, 127
 Peanut Butter Snacking Cake with Caramel Frosting, 61–62
 Peanut Butter Swiss Meringue Buttercream, 131
peanuts: Peanut Butter Cup Crunch, 107–108
pineapple: Carrot Pineapple Sheet Cake with Tangy Yogurt Frosting, 191
Pink Vanilla Frosting, 127
piping
 piping bag tips, 25
 styles/techniques, 26–30
 tools for, 12
pistachios
 Pistachio Cake with Strawberry Swiss Meringue Buttercream, 169–170
 Pistachio Cookie Moss, 155–157
 Pressed Flower Funfetti Cake Bars, 195–196
Pumpkin Pie Cake, Cozy, 52

R

rainbow sprinkles
 Funfetti Cake with Vanilla Buttercream and Birthday Cake Crumbles, 91–92
 Pressed Flower Funfetti Cake Bars, 195–196
raspberries
 Buttercream Flower Garden Holy Sheet Cake, 182–183

Chocolate Almond Brownie Cake with Vanilla Buttercream, 47–48
Coffee Milk Cake with Coffee Swiss Meringue Buttercream + Raspberries, 105–106
Matcha Green Tea Cake with Raspberry Swiss Meringue Buttercream + Matcha Mini Cookies, 161–162
Mocha Dacquoise Cake, 164–165
Party Time Chocolate Raspberry Ruffle Cake, 112–114
Raspberry Italian Meringue Buttercream, 137
Raspberry Lemon Sheet Cake with Raspberry Italian Meringue Buttercream, 199–200
Raspberry Swiss Meringue Buttercream, 131
Vanilla Almond Raspberry Cake with Vanilla Buttercream + Caramel Almond Brittle, 73–74
You Got Jammed (A Very Berry Quick Jam Recipe), 141

S

Salted Caramel, 126
Salted Caramel Buttercream, 126
sesame seeds: Black Sesame Brittle Cake with Coconut Swiss Meringue Buttercream, 159–160
sheet cakes
 Buttercream Flower Garden Holy Sheet Cake, 182–183
 Carrot Pineapple Sheet Cake with Tangy Yogurt Frosting, 191
 Coconut Haupia Cake with Passion Fruit Syrup, 187–188
 Pressed Flower Funfetti Cake Bars, 195–196
 Raspberry Lemon Sheet Cake with Raspberry Italian Meringue Buttercream, 199–200
 Tie-Dye Rainbow Piped Buttercream Cake, 201–202
Simple Vanilla Syrup, 169–170
soaks
 in cake making, 16
 Coffee Milk, 105–106
 Coffee Syrup, 149–150
 Vanilla Milk, 182–183

INDEX 231

sour cream, plant-based
   Blueberry Sour Cream Streusel Cake, 55–56
   Lemon Loaf Cake with Vanilla Bean Glaze, 51
soy milk, as ingredient, 6
strawberries
   Birthday Cupcakes with Strawberry Frosting, 207
   PB+J Chocolate Cake with Peanut Butter Cup Crunch, 107–108
   Pistachio Cake with Strawberry Swiss Meringue Buttercream, 169–170
   Strawberries and Cream Strawberry Jam Cake, 71
   Strawberry Buttercream, 127
   Strawberry Dream Cake with Strawberry Swiss Meringue Buttercream, 99–100
   Strawberry Swiss Meringue Buttercream, 132
   You Got Jammed (A Very Berry Quick Jam Recipe), 141
Streusel Cake, Blueberry Sour Cream, 55–56
Supermarket Bakery-Style Cake with Pink Vanilla Buttercream, 75–76
Swiss meringue buttercreams *see* buttercreams, Swiss meringue
syrups *see also* frostings; glazes
   in cake making, 16
   Earl Grey Tea, 151–152
   Lemon, 193–194
   Matcha, 161–162
   Passion Fruit, 89–90, 187–188
   Simple Vanilla, 169–170
   Vanilla, 195–196
   Vanilla Simple, 159–160

T

Tangy Yogurt Frosting, 140
tea
   Dance Like No One is Watching Earl Grey Cake with Lemon Italian Meringue Buttercream, 151–152
   Matcha Green Tea Cake with Raspberry Swiss Meringue Buttercream + Matcha Mini Cookies, 161–162

The "They Don't Know They're Healthy" Banana Chocolate Chip Cupcakes, 213–214
thickeners, in cake making, 7
Tie-Dye Rainbow Piped Buttercream Cake, 201–202
Toasted Coconut, 187–188
Toffee Bits, 151–152
Toffee Crunch, 85–86
tools, for cake making, 11–12

V

vanilla
   Birthday Cupcakes with Strawberry Frosting, 207
   Black Sesame Brittle Cake with Coconut Swiss Meringue Buttercream, 159–160
   Blackberry Almond Cupcakes with Vanilla Blackberry Jam Frosting, 208–209
   Buttercream Flower Garden Holy Sheet Cake, 182–183
   Chocolate Almond Brownie Cake with Vanilla Buttercream, 47–48
   Coconut Haupia Cake with Passion Fruit Syrup, 187–188
   Coffee Milk Cake with Coffee Swiss Meringue Buttercream + Raspberries, 105–106
   Cookies and Cream Cake, 101–102
   Fancy Breakfast Cake with Maple Italian Meringue Buttercream, Coffee Syrup + Blueberry Jam, 149–150
   Funfetti Cake with Vanilla Buttercream and Birthday Cake Crumbles, 91–92
   Garden Party Vanilla Lemon Cupcakes, 210
   Giant Chocolate Chip Cookie Cake with Vanilla Buttercream, 145–146
   as ingredient, 7
   Lemon Loaf Cake with Vanilla Bean Glaze, 51
   Abstract-Painted Buttercream Blackberry Cake with Meringue Kisses, 177–179
   Passion Fruit Vanilla Bean Ombré Cake with Caramel Crunch, 89–90

   Passion Fruit Vanilla Swiss Meringue Buttercream, 132
   Pink Vanilla Frosting, 127
   Pressed Flower Funfetti Cake Bars, 195–196
   Strawberries and Cream Strawberry Jam Cake, 71
   Supermarket Bakery-Style Cake with Pink Vanilla Buttercream, 75–76
   Tie-Dye Rainbow Piped Buttercream Cake, 201–202
   Vanilla Almond Raspberry Cake with Vanilla Buttercream + Caramel Almond Brittle, 73–74
   Vanilla Bean Buttercream, 125
   Vanilla Buttercream, 125
   Vanilla Cake with Coffee Icing Glaze, 63–64
   Vanilla Fruit + Flowers Cake with Vanilla Bean Swiss Meringue Buttercream, 95–96
   Vanilla Italian Meringue Buttercream, 136
   Vanilla Simple Syrup, 159–160
   Vanilla Swiss Meringue Buttercream, 130
   Vanilla Syrup, 195–196
vegetable shortening, as ingredient, 7
Versawhip powder
   uses for, 9
   Versawhip Meringue for Italian Buttercream, 136
   Versawhip Meringue for Swiss Meringue Buttercream, 130

W

whipped creams
   Coconut Whipped Cream, 52
   Maple Coconut Whipped Cream, 45–46
   Whipped Coconut Cream, 187–188

Y

yogurt
   as ingredient, 7
   Tangy Yogurt Frosting, 140
You Got Jammed (A Very Berry Quick Jam Recipe), 141